Kenneth Grahame
The Wind in The Willows

adapted by
Michel Plessix

Vol. 4
Panic at Toad Hall

NANTIER · BEALL · MINOUSTCHINE
Publishing inc.
new york

Also available:
The Wind in the Willows:
volumes 1, 2, 3: $15.95 each
by Will Eisner:
The Last Knight: $15.95 hc, $7.95 pb
Moby Dick: $15.95 hc, $7.95 pb
The Princess & The Frog: $15.95
by P. Craig Russell:
The Fairy Tales of Oscar Wilde:
volumes 1, 2, 3: $15.95 each
Jungle Book: $16.95
The Fairy Tales of the Brothers Grimm: $15.95
Peter and the Wolf: $15.95

(add $3 P&H first item, $1 each addt'l)

ISBN 1-56163-311-9

Translation by Joe Johnson
Lettering by Michael Wood
Printed in France

Kenneth Grahame
The Wind in The Willows
adapted by
Michel Plessix
Vol. 1
The Wild Wood

Kenneth Grahame
The Wind in The Willows
adapted by
Michel Plessix
Vol. 2
Mr. Toad

Kenneth Grahame
The Wind in The Willows
adapted by
Michel Plessix
Vol. 3
The Gates of Dawn

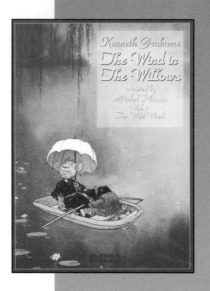

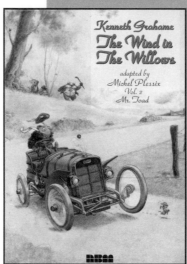

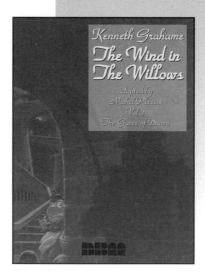

Chapter X

"Like Summer Tempests Came His Tears"

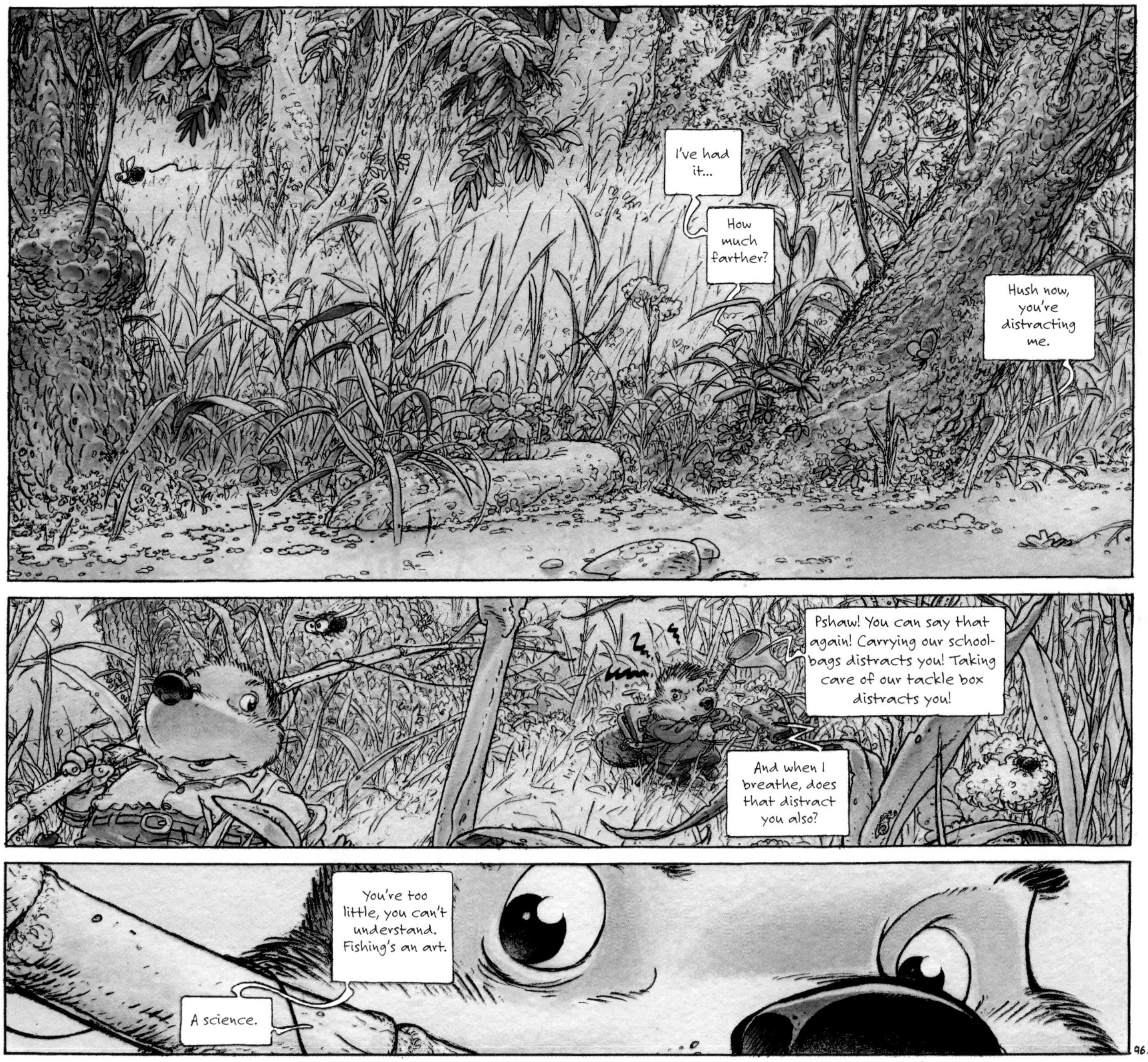
I've had it...
How much farther?
Hush now, you're distracting me.
Pshaw! You can say that again! Carrying our school-bags distracts you! Taking care of our tackle box distracts you!
And when I breathe, does that distract you also?
You're too little, you can't understand. Fishing's an art.
A science.
96

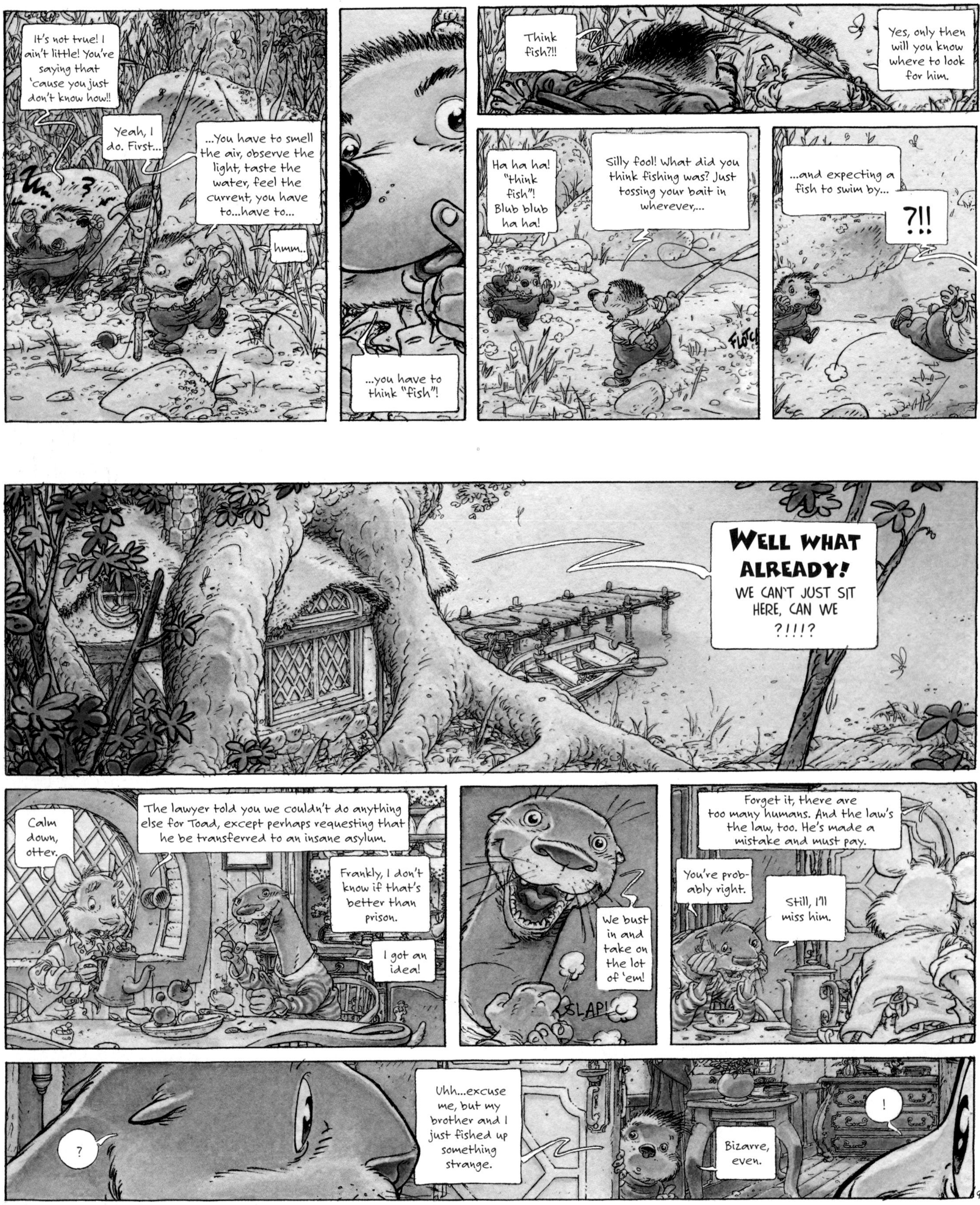
It's not true! I ain't little! You're saying that 'cause you just don't know how!!
Yeah, I do. First...
...You have to smell the air, observe the light, taste the water, feel the current, you have to...have to...
hmm..
...you have to think "fish"!
Think fish?!!
Yes, only then will you know where to look for him.
Ha ha ha! "think fish"! Blub blub ha ha!
Silly fool! What did you think fishing was? Just tossing your bait in wherever,...
FLOTCH
...and expecting a fish to swim by...
?!!
WELL WHAT ALREADY!
WE CAN'T JUST SIT HERE, CAN WE ?!!!?
Calm down, otter.
The lawyer told you we couldn't do anything else for Toad, except perhaps requesting that he be transferred to an insane asylum.
Frankly, I don't know if that's better than prison.
I got an idea!
We bust in and take on the lot of 'em!
SLAP!
Forget it, there are too many humans. And the law's the law, too. He's made a mistake and must pay.
You're probably right.
Still, I'll miss him.
?
Uhh...excuse me, but my brother and I just fished up something strange.
Bizarre, even.
!

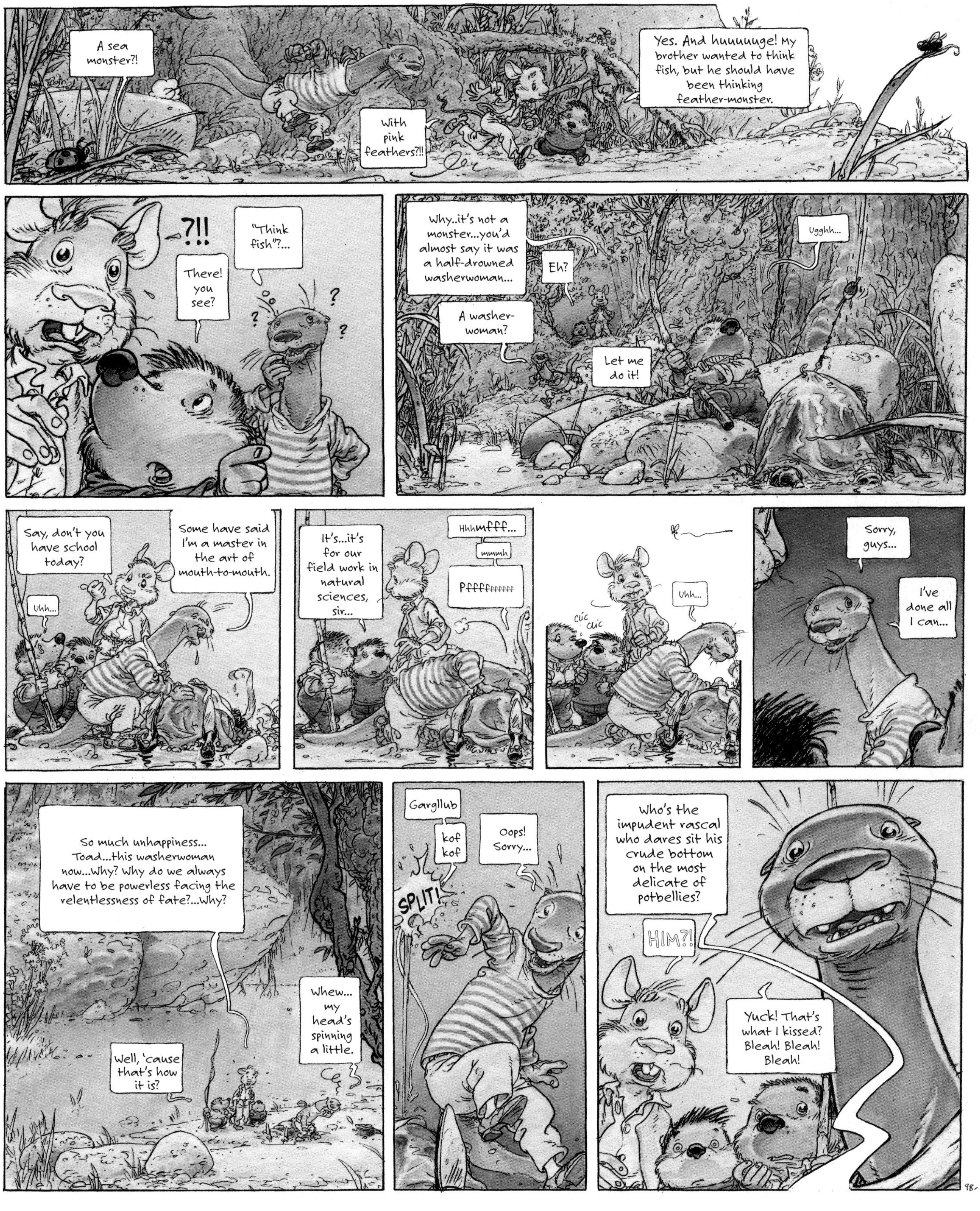

A sea monster?!
With pink feathers?!!
Yes. And huuuuuge! My brother wanted to think fish, but he should have been thinking feather-monster.
?!!
There! you see?
“Think fish”?...
Why..it's not a monster...you'd almost say it was a half-drowned washerwoman...
Eh?
Ugghh...
A washer-woman?
Let me do it!
Say, don't you have school today?
Some have said I'm a master in the art of mouth-to-mouth.
Uhh...
It's...it's for our field work in natural sciences, sir...
Hhhmfff...
mmmh
Pfffffffff
Clic clic
Uhh...
Sorry, guys...
I've done all I can...
So much unhappiness... Toad...this washerwoman now...Why? Why do we always have to be powerless facing the relentlessness of fate?...Why?
Whew... my head's spinning a little.
Well, 'cause that's how it is?
Gargllub
kof kof
Oops! Sorry...
SPLIT!
Who's the impudent rascal who dares sit his crude bottom on the most delicate of potbellies?
HIM?!
Yuck! That's what I kissed? Bleah! Bleah! Bleah!

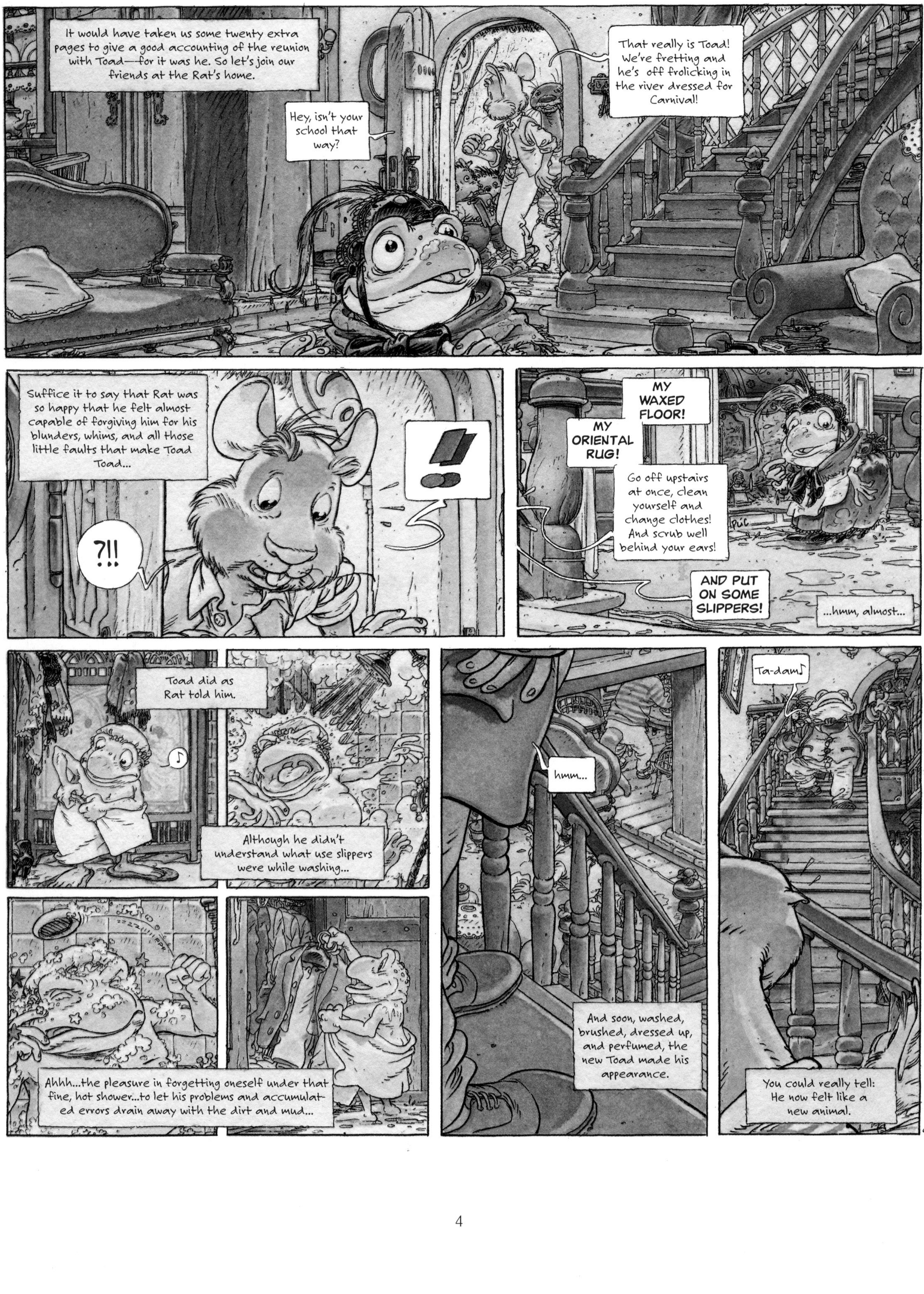
It would have taken us some twenty extra pages to give a good accounting of the reunion with Toad—for it was he. So let's join our friends at the Rat's home.
Hey, isn't your school that way?
That really is Toad! We're fretting and he's off frolicking in the river dressed for Carnival!
Suffice it to say that Rat was so happy that he felt almost capable of forgiving him for his blunders, whims, and all those little faults that make Toad Toad...
?!!
MY WAXED FLOOR!
MY ORIENTAL RUG!
Go off upstairs at once, clean yourself and change clothes! And scrub well behind your ears!
AND PUT ON SOME SLIPPERS!
...hmm, almost...
Toad did as Rat told him.
♪
Although he didn't understand what use slippers were while washing...
Ahhh...the pleasure in forgetting oneself under that fine, hot shower...to let his problems and accumulated errors drain away with the dirt and mud...
hmm...
And soon, washed, brushed, dressed up, and perfumed, the new Toad made his appearance.
Ta-dam♪
You could really tell: He now felt like a new animal.

We've made a snack for you like you haven't had for a long time.

Come have something to eat while telling us of your adventures. I'm guessing you must have good stories full of brawls!

Lots of good things: bergamot tea, baked apples, copiously buttered toast and muffins...

Sorry, I don't have any more orange marmalade.

And Toad set to eating, eating, eating; to talking, talking, talking; to spluttering, too. And especially to boasting.

Yesh, yesh, I assure you! A horde of a hundred-fifty furioush shailors!

Noooo...

It's incredible...

Isn't it?

Humph!

What's incredible is that none of your misadventures has taught you a lesson! What a braggart you are! I'm sure that at the first backfire, you'll start again...

Think of your friends! I don't want you to go back to prison!

Do you think it's any pleasure for me to hear it said that I'm the chap that keeps company with jailbirds?!!

!

Well...

Gulp.

As always, you're right. No more cars and inopportune driving...

The fact is, just now, while I was drowning, I had a sudden idea connected with motorboats and...

I got it! He was thinking fish!!

okay. You're quite right. From now on, I'll be good and peaceful and worry about my roses, keep a pony-chaise and all those things that make up the life of a gentleman of property...

It'll be wonderful...

Yippee.

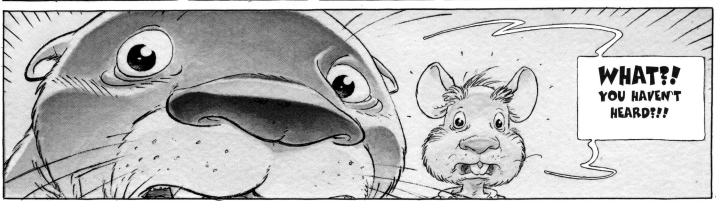

WHAT?! YOU HAVEN'T HEARD!!!

5

Heard what? You're starting to worry me.

You should.

...

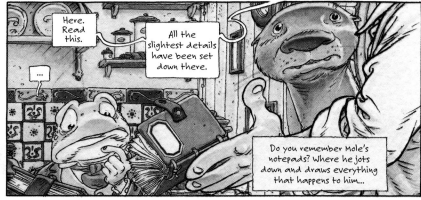

Here. Read this.

All the slightest details have been set down there.

Do you remember Mole's notepads? Where he jots down and draws everything that happens to him...

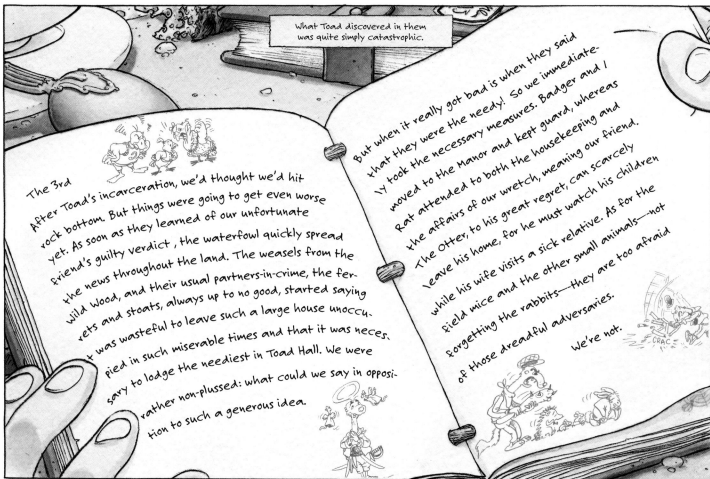

What Toad discovered in them was quite simply catastrophic.

The 3rd

After Toad's incarceration, we'd thought we'd hit rock bottom. But things were going to get even worse yet. As soon as they learned of our unfortunate friend's guilty verdict, the waterfowl quickly spread the news throughout the land. The weasels from the Wild Wood, and their usual partners-in-crime, the ferrets and stoats, always up to no good, started saying it was wasteful to leave such a large house unoccupied in such miserable times and that it was necessary to lodge the neediest in Toad Hall. We were rather non-plussed: what could we say in opposition to such a generous idea.

But when it really got bad is when they said that they were the needy! So we immediately took the necessary measures. Badger and I moved to the Manor and kept guard, whereas Rat attended to both the housekeeping and the affairs of our wretch, meaning our friend. The Otter, to his great regret, can scarcely leave his home, for he must watch his children while his wife visits a sick relative. As for the field mice and the other small animals—not forgetting the rabbits—they are too afraid of those dreadful adversaries.

We're not.

CRAC

As he went along in his reading, the Toad persuaded himself that some terrible, irreparable, no doubt irreversible thing was going to occur. He then felt his tears irrepressibly rising within himself...

Did you see the little drawings?

Funny, no?

101

6

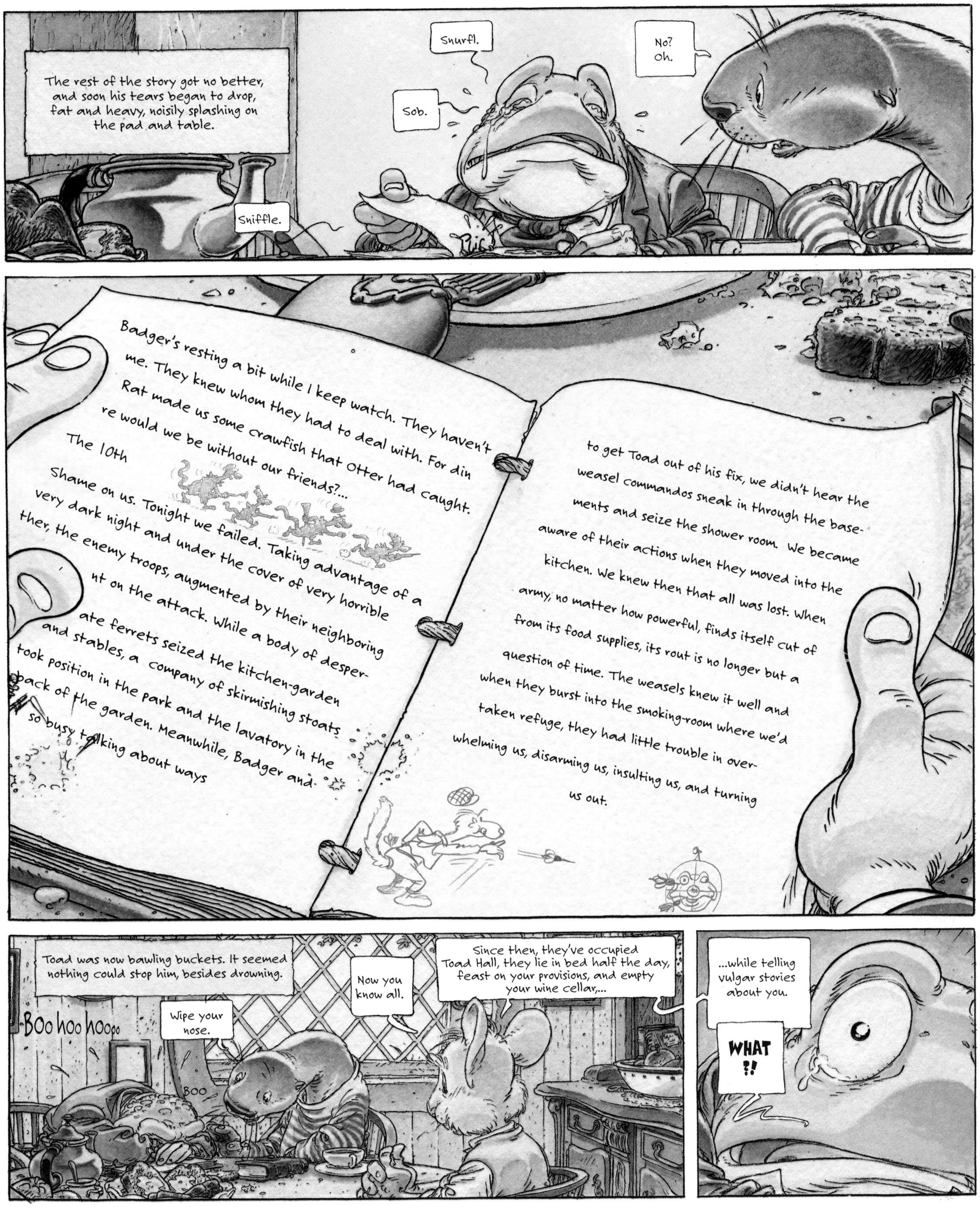

The rest of the story got no better, and soon his tears began to drop, fat and heavy, noisily splashing on the pad and table.
Sniffle.
Sob.
Snurfl.
No? Oh.
Badger's resting a bit while I keep watch. They haven't
me. They knew whom they had to deal with. For din
Rat made us some crawfish that Otter had caught.
re would we be without our friends?...
The 10th
Shame on us. Tonight we failed. Taking advantage of a
very dark night and under the cover of very horrible
ther, the enemy troops, augmented by their neighboring
nt on the attack. While a body of desper-
ate ferrets seized the kitchen-garden
and stables, a company of skirmishing stoats
took position in the park and the lavatory in the
back of the garden. Meanwhile, Badger and
so busy talking about ways
to get Toad out of his fix, we didn't hear the
weasel commandos sneak in through the base-
ments and seize the shower room. We became
aware of their actions when they moved into the
kitchen. We knew then that all was lost. When
army, no matter how powerful, finds itself cut of
from its food supplies, its rout is no longer but a
question of time. The weasels knew it well and
when they burst into the smoking-room where we'd
taken refuge, they had little trouble in over-
whelming us, disarming us, insulting us, and turning
us out.
Toad was now bawling buckets. It seemed nothing could stop him, besides drowning.
BOO hoo hoooo
Wipe your nose.
BOO
Now you know all.
Since then, they've occupied Toad Hall, they lie in bed half the day, feast on your provisions, and empty your wine cellar,...
...while telling vulgar stories about you.
WHAT ?!

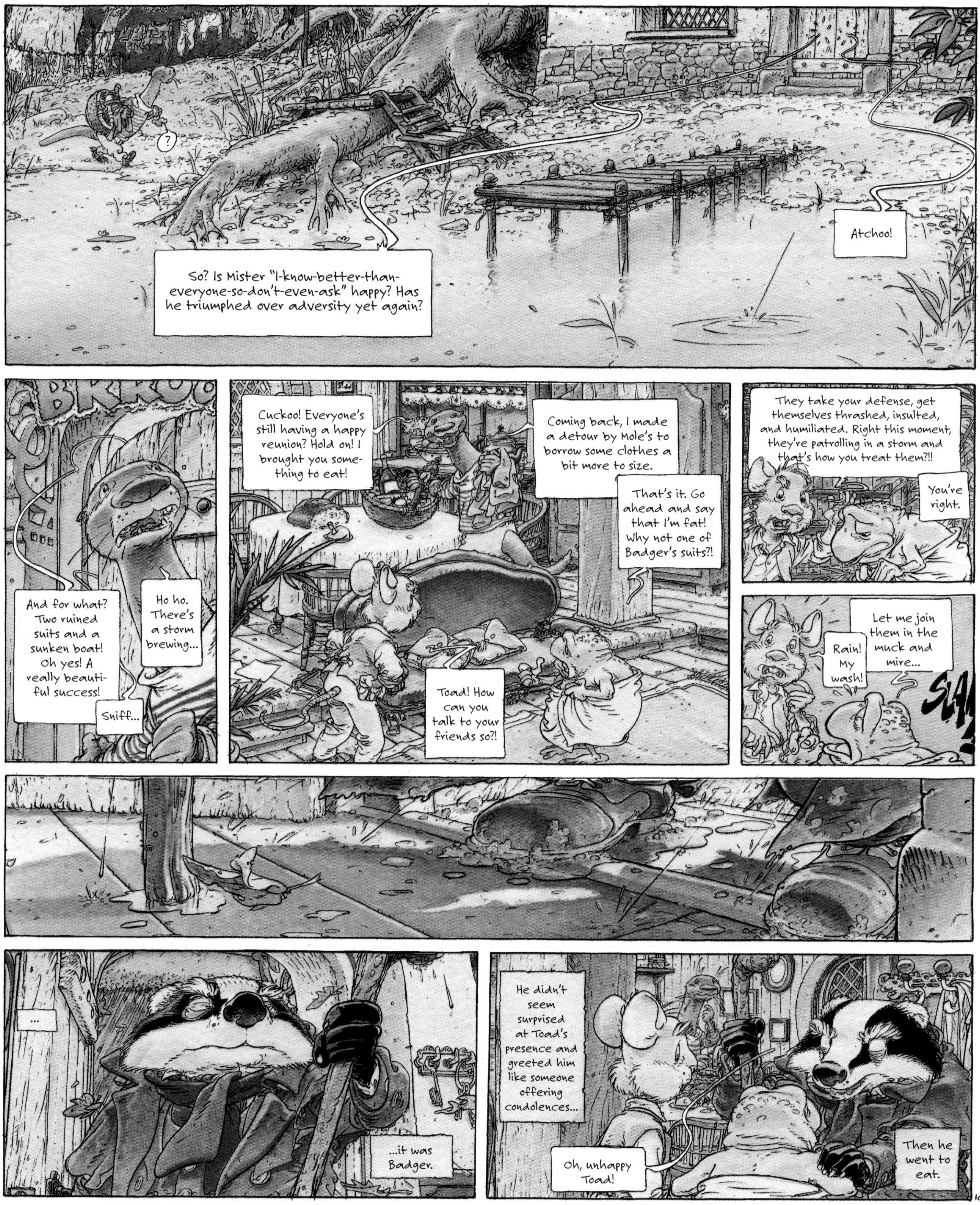
?
So? Is Mister "I-know-better-than-everyone-so-don't-even-ask" happy? Has he triumphed over adversity yet again?
Atchoo!
And for what? Two ruined suits and a sunken boat! Oh yes! A really beautiful success!
Ho ho. There's a storm brewing...
Sniff...
Cuckoo! Everyone's still having a happy reunion? Hold on! I brought you something to eat!
Coming back, I made a detour by Mole's to borrow some clothes a bit more to size.
That's it. Go ahead and say that I'm fat! Why not one of Badger's suits?!
Toad! How can you talk to your friends so?!
They take your defense, get themselves thrashed, insulted, and humiliated. Right this moment, they're patrolling in a storm and that's how you treat them?!!
You're right.
Rain! My wash!
Let me join them in the muck and mire...
...
...it was Badger.
He didn't seem surprised at Toad's presence and greeted him like someone offering condolences...
Oh, unhappy Toad!
Then he went to eat.

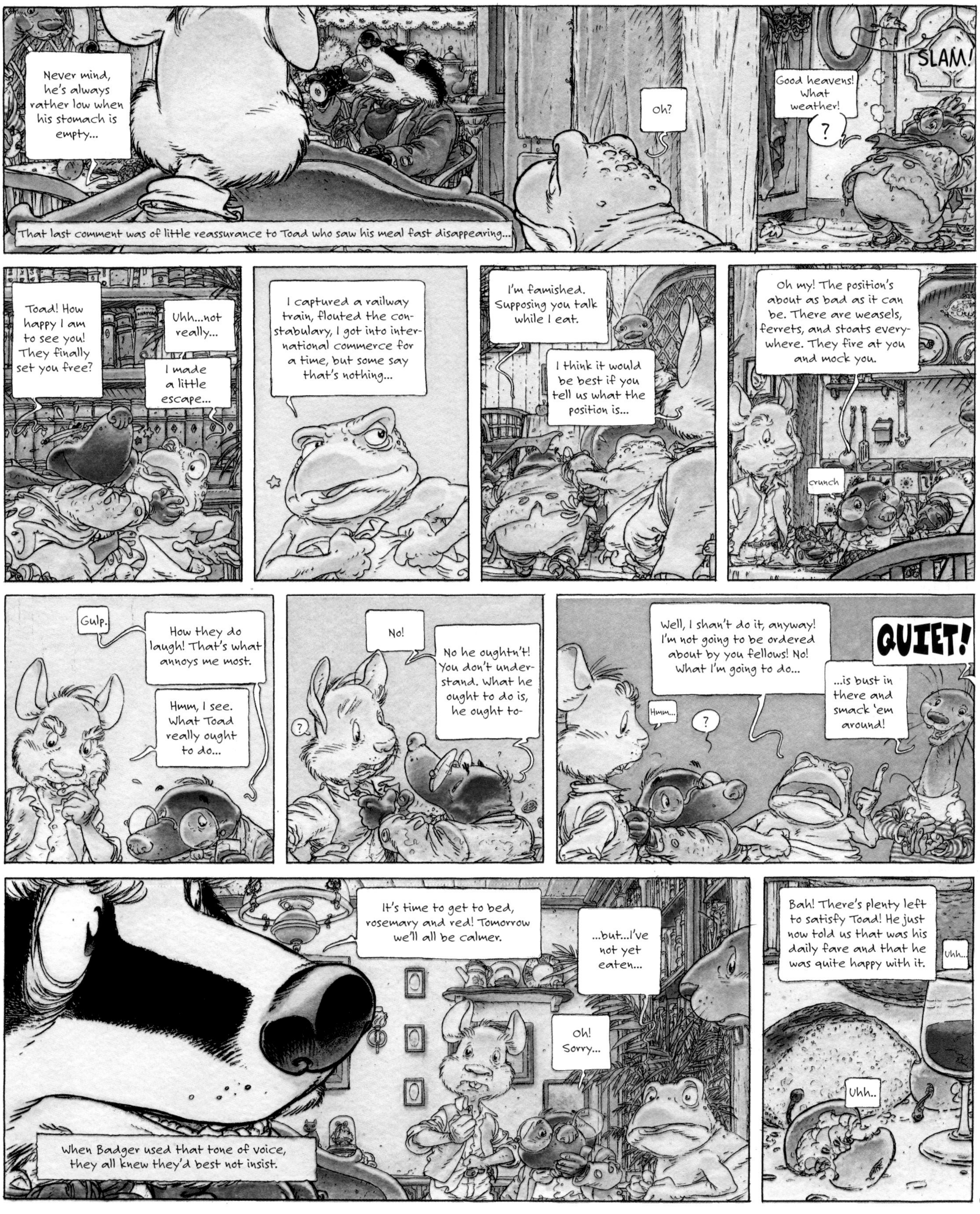

Never mind, he's always rather low when his stomach is empty...
That last comment was of little reassurance to Toad who saw his meal fast disappearing...
Oh?
SLAM!
Good heavens! What weather!
?
Toad! How happy I am to see you! They finally set you free?
Uhh...not really...
I made a little escape...
I captured a railway train, flouted the constabulary, I got into international commerce for a time, but some say that's nothing...
I'm famished. Supposing you talk while I eat.
I think it would be best if you tell us what the position is...
Oh my! The position's about as bad as it can be. There are weasels, ferrets, and stoats everywhere. They fire at you and mock you.
crunch
Gulp.
How they do laugh! That's what annoys me most.
Hmm, I see. What Toad really ought to do...
No!
?
No he oughtn't! You don't understand. What he ought to do is, he ought to-
Well, I shan't do it, anyway! I'm not going to be ordered about by you fellows! No! What I'm going to do...
Hmm...
?
...is bust in there and smack 'em around!
QUIET!
It's time to get to bed, rosemary and red! Tomorrow we'll all be calmer.
...but...I've not yet eaten...
Oh! Sorry...
When Badger used that tone of voice, they all knew they'd best not insist.
Bah! There's plenty left to satisfy Toad! He just now told us that was his daily fare and that he was quite happy with it.
Uhh...
Uhh..

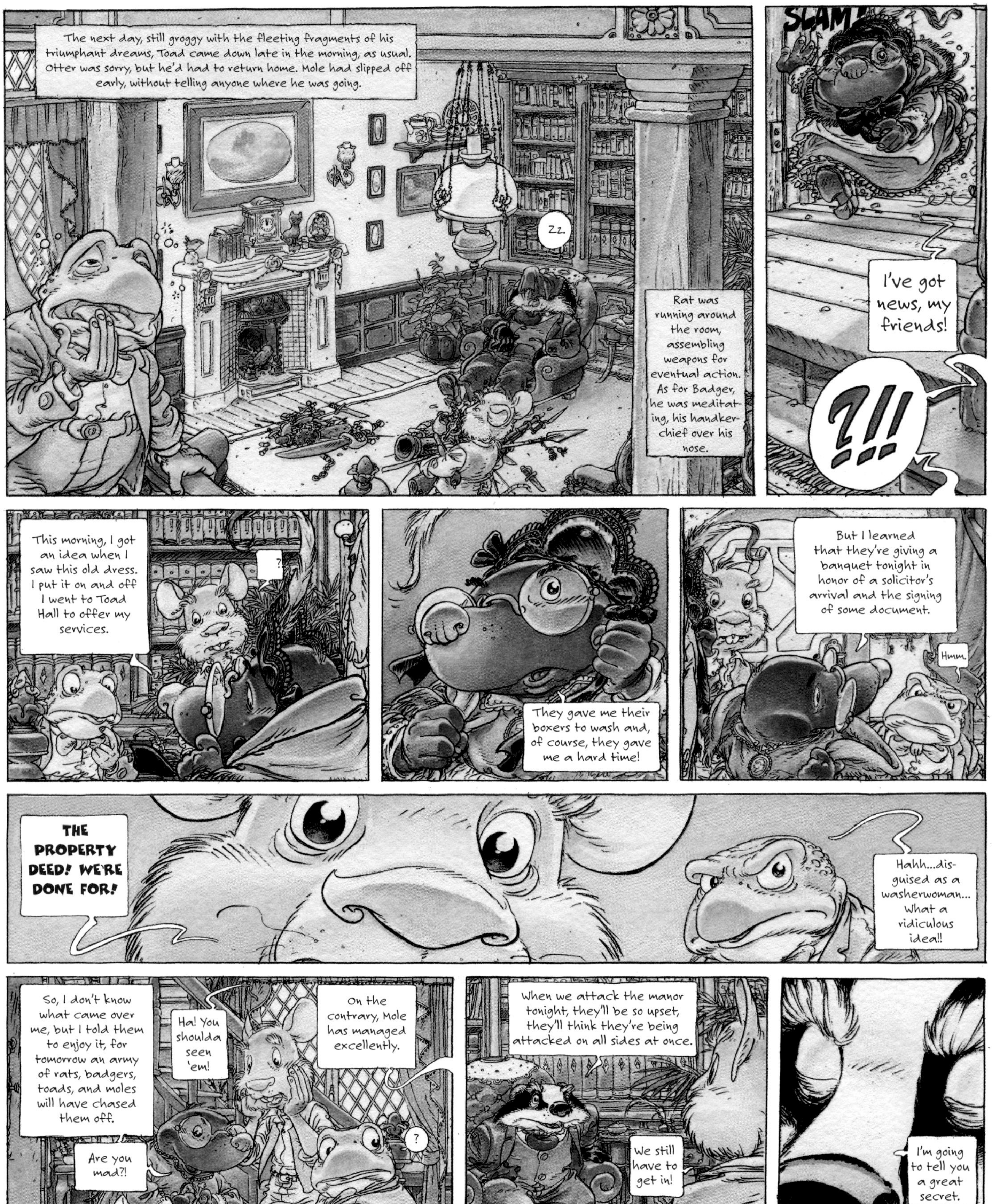
The next day, still groggy with the fleeting fragments of his triumphant dreams, Toad came down late in the morning, as usual. Otter was sorry, but he'd had to return home. Mole had slipped off early, without telling anyone where he was going.
Zz.
Rat was running around the room, assembling weapons for eventual action. As for Badger, he was meditating, his handkerchief over his nose.
SLAM!
I've got news, my friends!
?!!
This morning, I got an idea when I saw this old dress. I put it on and off I went to Toad Hall to offer my services.
?
They gave me their boxers to wash and, of course, they gave me a hard time!
But I learned that they're giving a banquet tonight in honor of a solicitor's arrival and the signing of some document.
Hmm.
THE PROPERTY DEED! WE'RE DONE FOR!
Hahh...disguised as a washerwoman... What a ridiculous idea!!
So, I don't know what came over me, but I told them to enjoy it, for tomorrow an army of rats, badgers, toads, and moles will have chased them off.
Ha! You shoulda seen 'em!
On the contrary, Mole has managed excellently.
Are you mad?!
?
When we attack the manor tonight, they'll be so upset, they'll think they're being attacked on all sides at once.
We still have to get in!
I'm going to tell you a great secret.

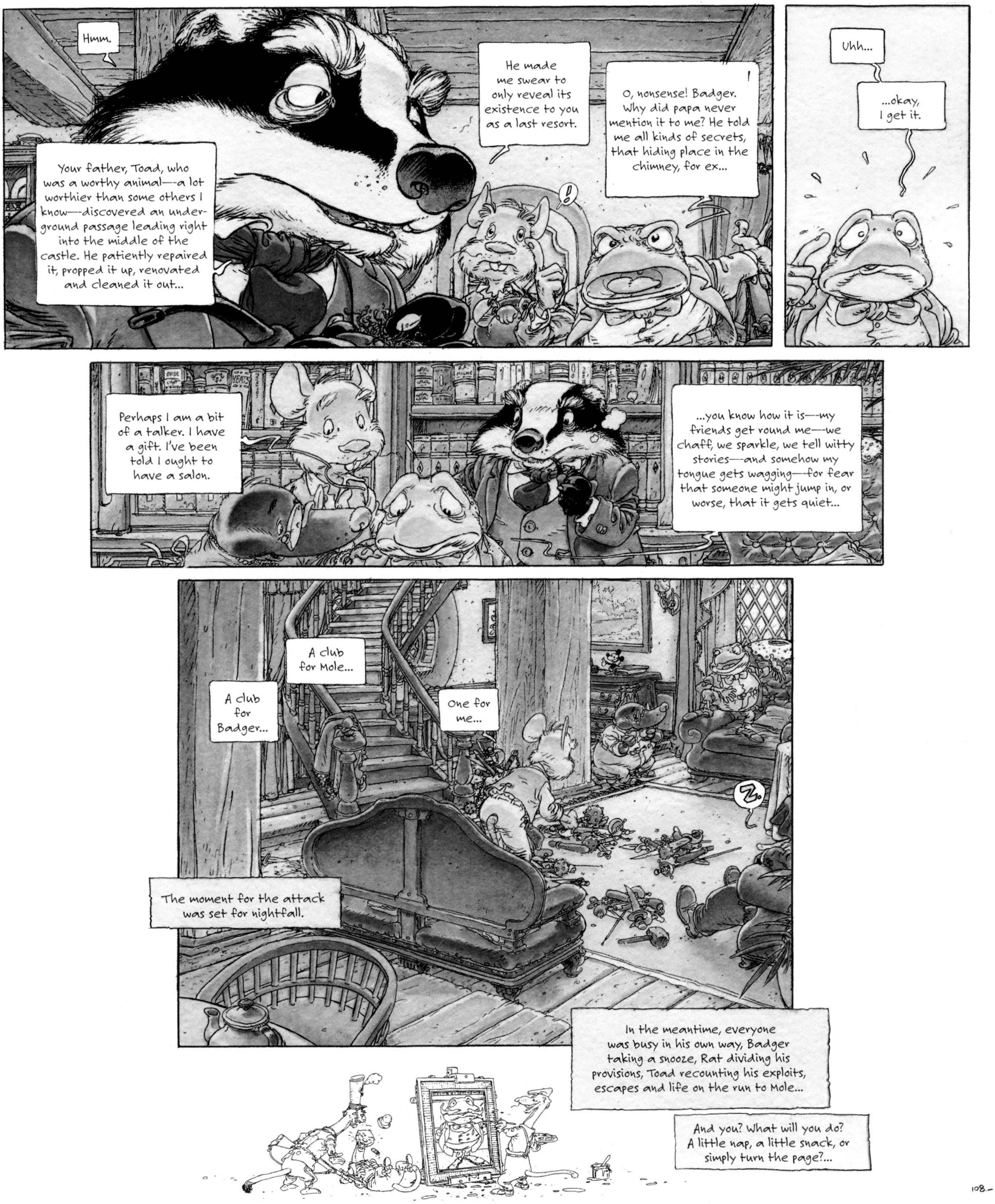
Hmm.
Your father, Toad, who was a worthy animal—a lot worthier than some others I know—discovered an underground passage leading right into the middle of the castle. He patiently repaired it, propped it up, renovated and cleaned it out...
He made me swear to only reveal its existence to you as a last resort.
!
O, nonsense! Badger. Why did papa never mention it to me? He told me all kinds of secrets, that hiding place in the chimney, for ex...
!
Uhh...
...okay, I get it.
Perhaps I am a bit of a talker. I have a gift. I've been told I ought to have a salon.
...you know how it is—my friends get round me—we chaff, we sparkle, we tell witty stories—and somehow my tongue gets wagging—for fear that someone might jump in, or worse, that it gets quiet...
A club for Badger...
A club for Mole...
One for me...
Z
The moment for the attack was set for nightfall.
In the meantime, everyone was busy in his own way, Badger taking a snooze, Rat dividing his provisions, Toad recounting his exploits, escapes and life on the run to Mole...
And you? What will you do? A little nap, a little snack, or simply turn the page?...
108-

Chapter XI

The Return of Ulysses

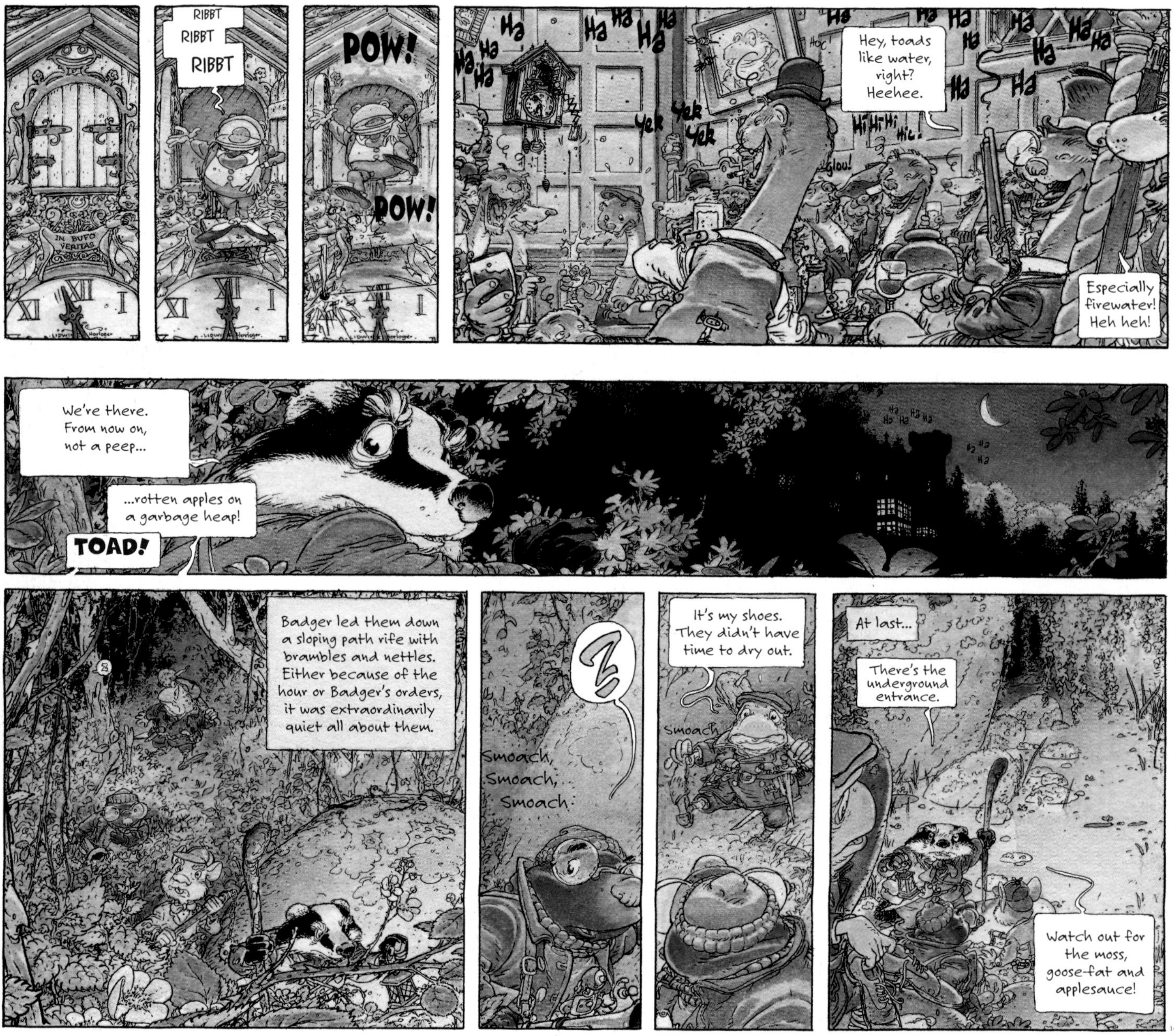

IN BUFO VERITAS
RIBBT
RIBBT
RIBBT
POW!
POW!
Hey, toads like water, right? Heehee.
Especially firewater! Heh heh!
We're there. From now on, not a peep...
...rotten apples on a garbage heap!
TOAD!
Badger led them down a sloping path rife with brambles and nettles. Either because of the hour or Badger's orders, it was extraordinarily quiet all about them.
Z
Smoach, Smoach, Smoach
It's my shoes. They didn't have time to dry out.
Smoach
At last...
There's the underground entrance.
Watch out for the moss, goose-fat and applesauce!

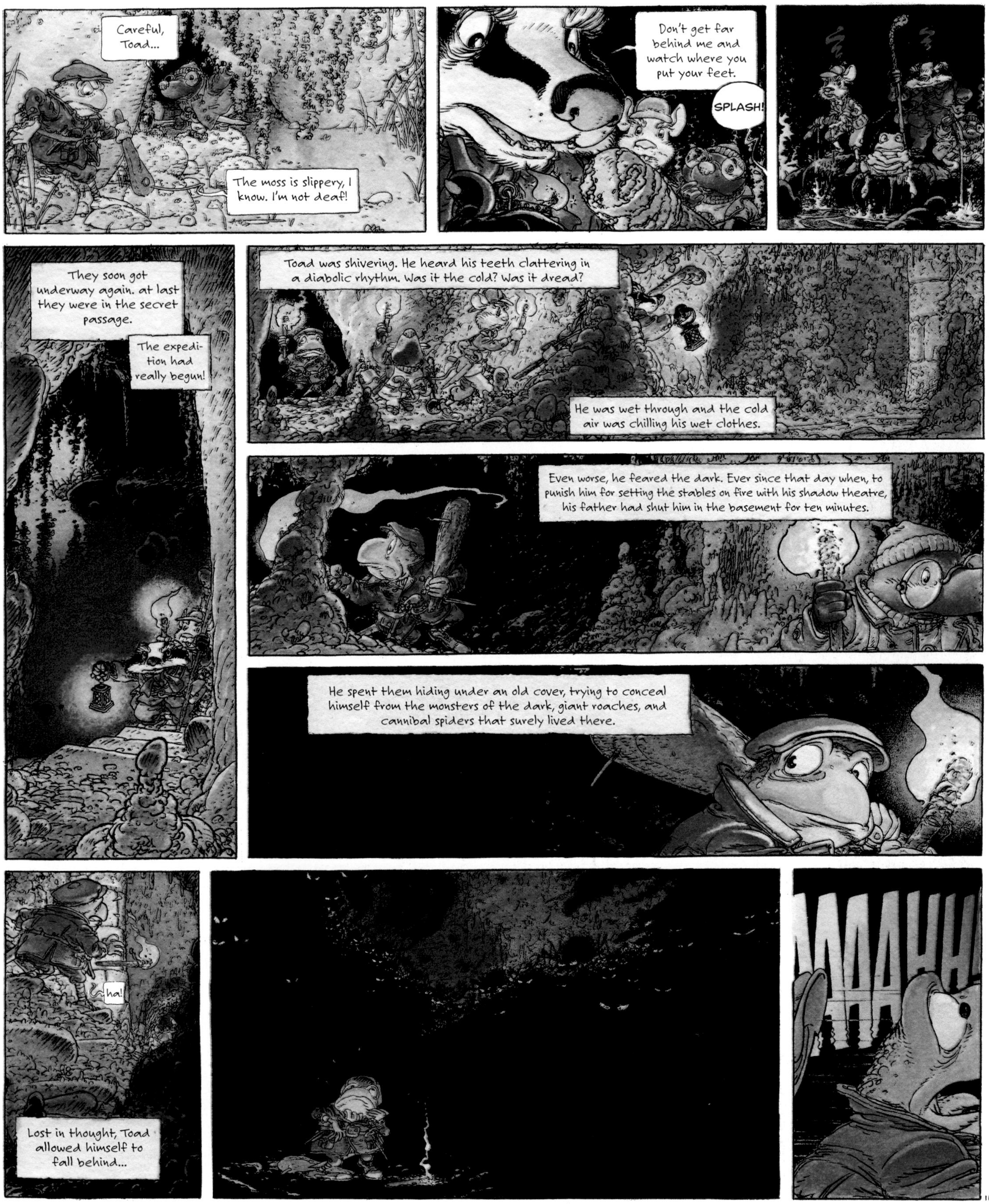

Careful, Toad...
The moss is slippery, I know. I'm not deaf!
Don't get far behind me and watch where you put your feet.
SPLASH!
They soon got underway again. at last they were in the secret passage.
The expedition had really begun!
Toad was shivering. He heard his teeth clattering in a diabolic rhythm. Was it the cold? Was it dread?
He was wet through and the cold air was chilling his wet clothes.
Even worse, he feared the dark. Ever since that day when, to punish him for setting the stables on fire with his shadow theatre, his father had shut him in the basement for ten minutes.
He spent them hiding under an old cover, trying to conceal himself from the monsters of the dark, giant roaches, and cannibal spiders that surely lived there.
ha!
Lost in thought, Toad allowed himself to fall behind...
AAAAHH

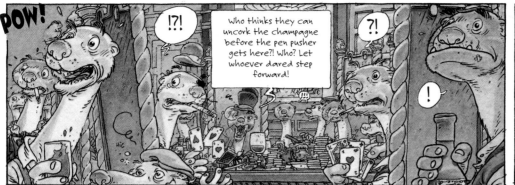

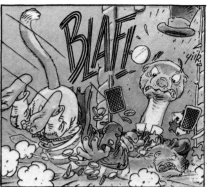

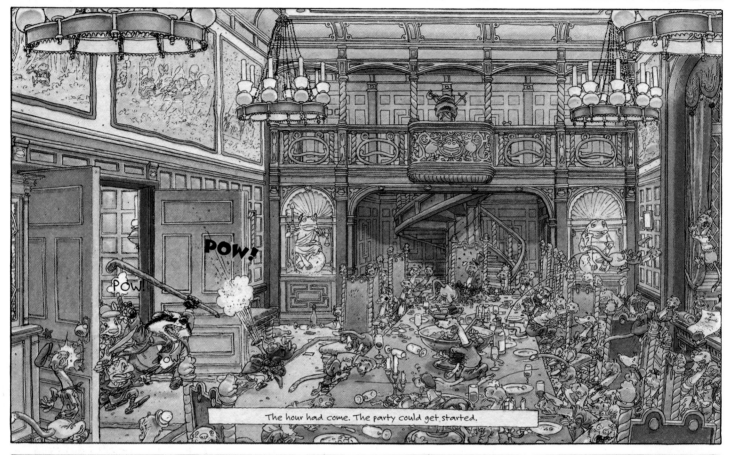

POW!
!?!
Who thinks they can uncork the champagne before the pen pusher gets here?! Who? Let whoever dared step forward!
?!
!
BLAF!
POW!
POW!
The hour had come. The party could get started.
GL.
It was a great brawl!
It was too bad that Otter was stuck home for family reasons!

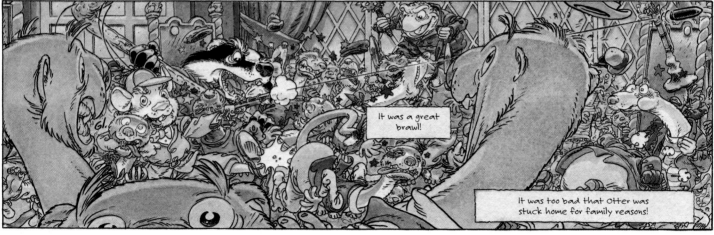

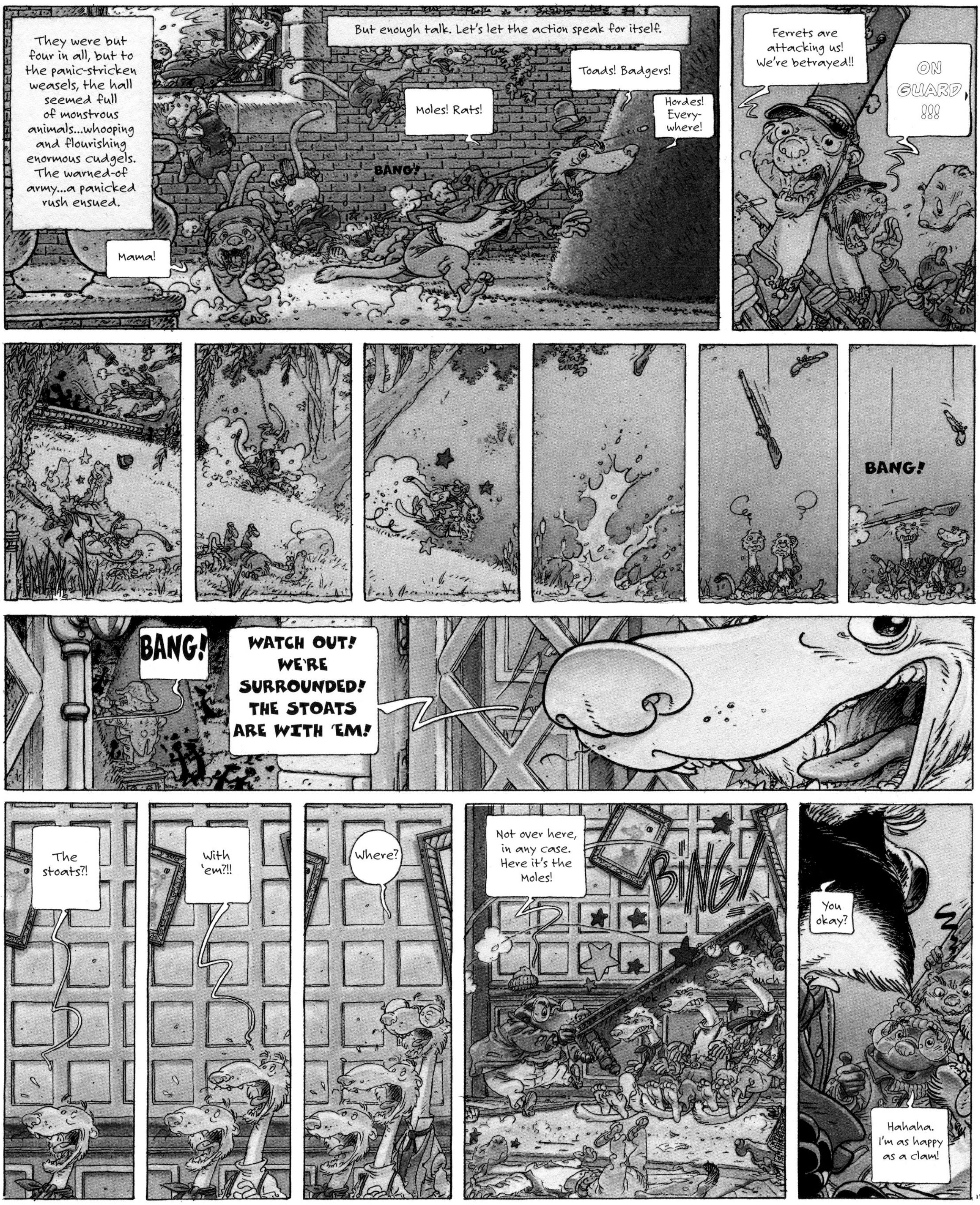
They were but four in all, but to the panic-stricken weasels, the hall seemed full of monstrous animals...whooping and flourishing enormous cudgels. The warned-of army...a panicked rush ensued.
But enough talk. Let's let the action speak for itself.
Moles! Rats!
Toads! Badgers!
Hordes! Every-where!
BANG!
Mama!
Ferrets are attacking us! We're betrayed!!
ON GUARD!!!
BANG!
BANG!
WATCH OUT! WE'RE SURROUNDED! THE STOATS ARE WITH 'EM!
The stoats?!
With 'em?!!
Where?
Not over here, in any case. Here it's the Moles!
BING!
You okay?
Hahaha. I'm as happy as a clam!

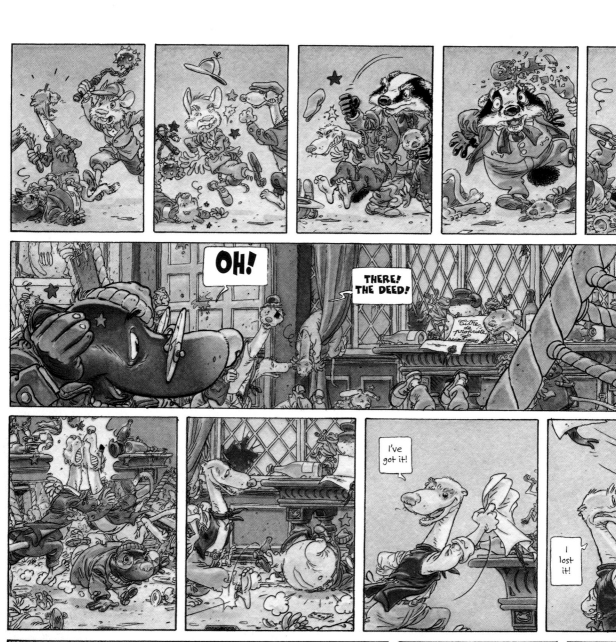

Oops, sorry...

OH!

THERE! THE DEED!

I've got it!

I lost it!

oh no!

oh yes!

Hup!

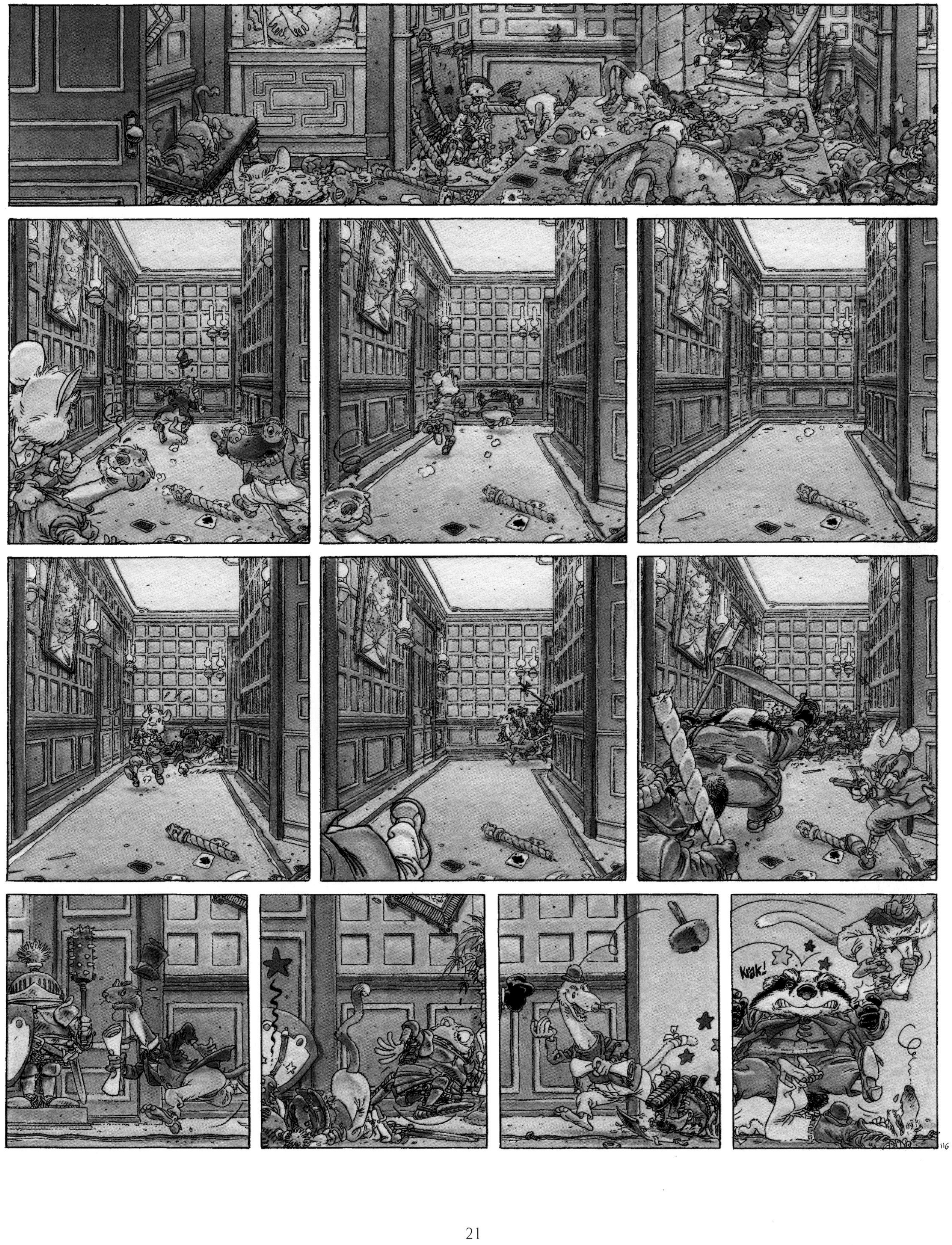
Krak!

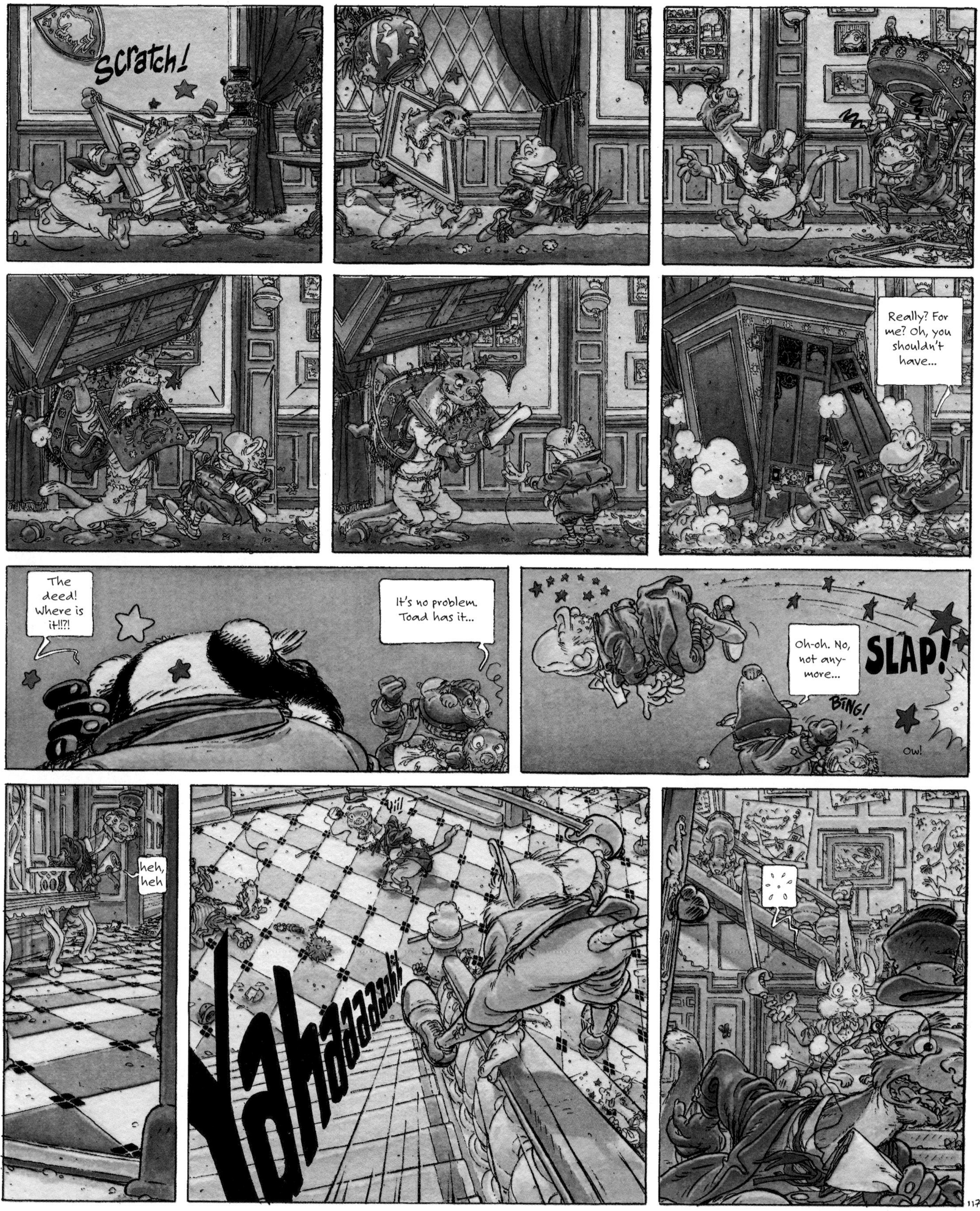
SCRATCH!
Really? For me? Oh, you shouldn't have...
The deed! Where is it!!?!
It's no problem. Toad has it...
Oh-oh. No, not any-more...
SLAP!
BING!
OW!
heh, heh
Yii!
Yahaaaaaaahh

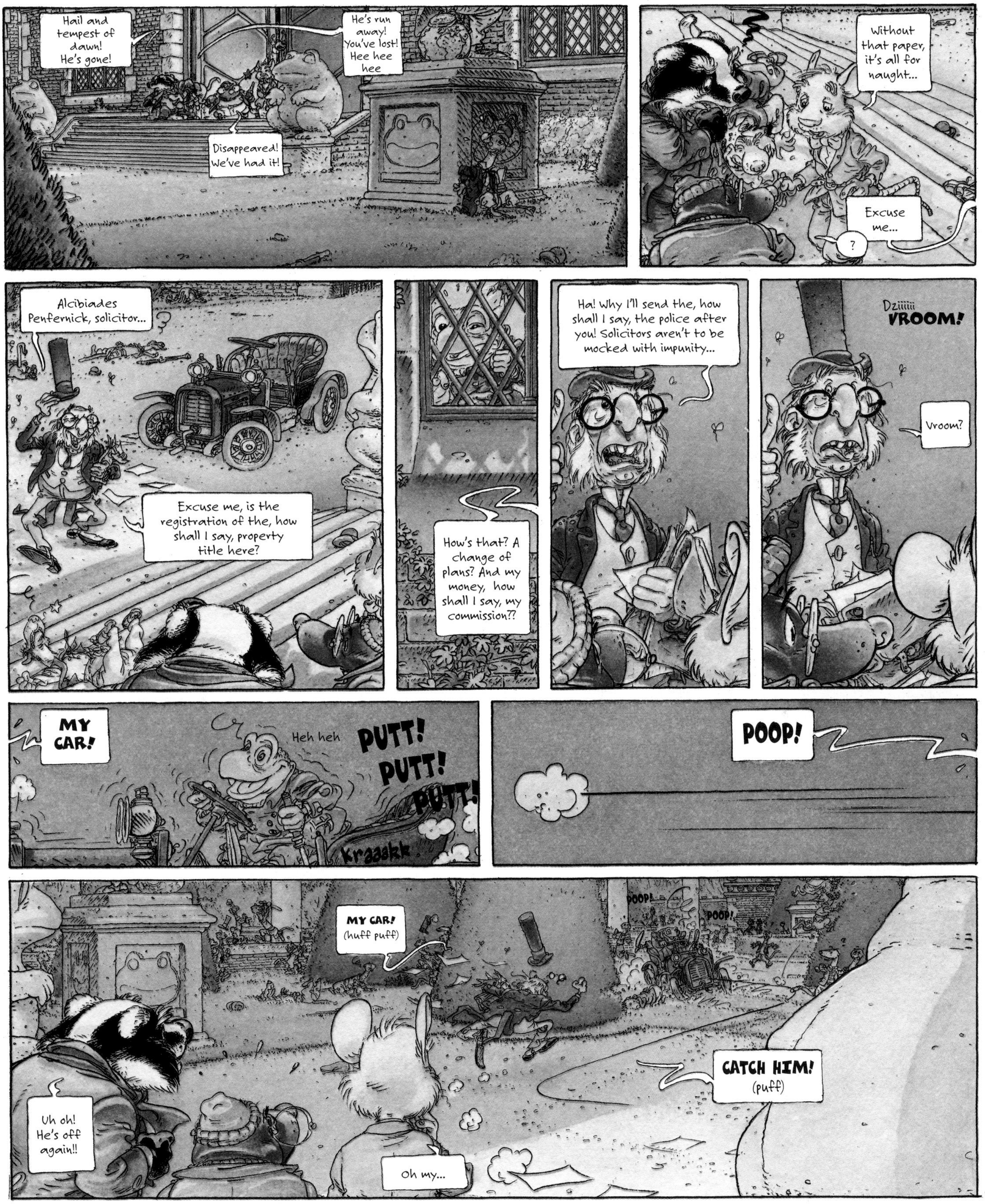
Hail and tempest of dawn! He's gone!
He's run away! You've lost! Hee hee hee
Disappeared! We've had it!
Without that paper, it's all for naught...
Excuse me...
?
Alcibiades Penfernick, solicitor...
Excuse me, is the registration of the, how shall I say, property title here?
How's that? A change of plans? And my money, how shall I say, my commission??
Ha! Why I'll send the, how shall I say, the police after you! Solicitors aren't to be mocked with impunity...
Dziiiiii VROOM!
Vroom?
MY CAR!
Heh heh
PUTT! PUTT! PUTT!
Kraaakk
POOP!
MY CAR! (huff puff)
POOP!
POOP!
CATCH HIM! (puff)
Uh oh! He's off again!!
Oh my...

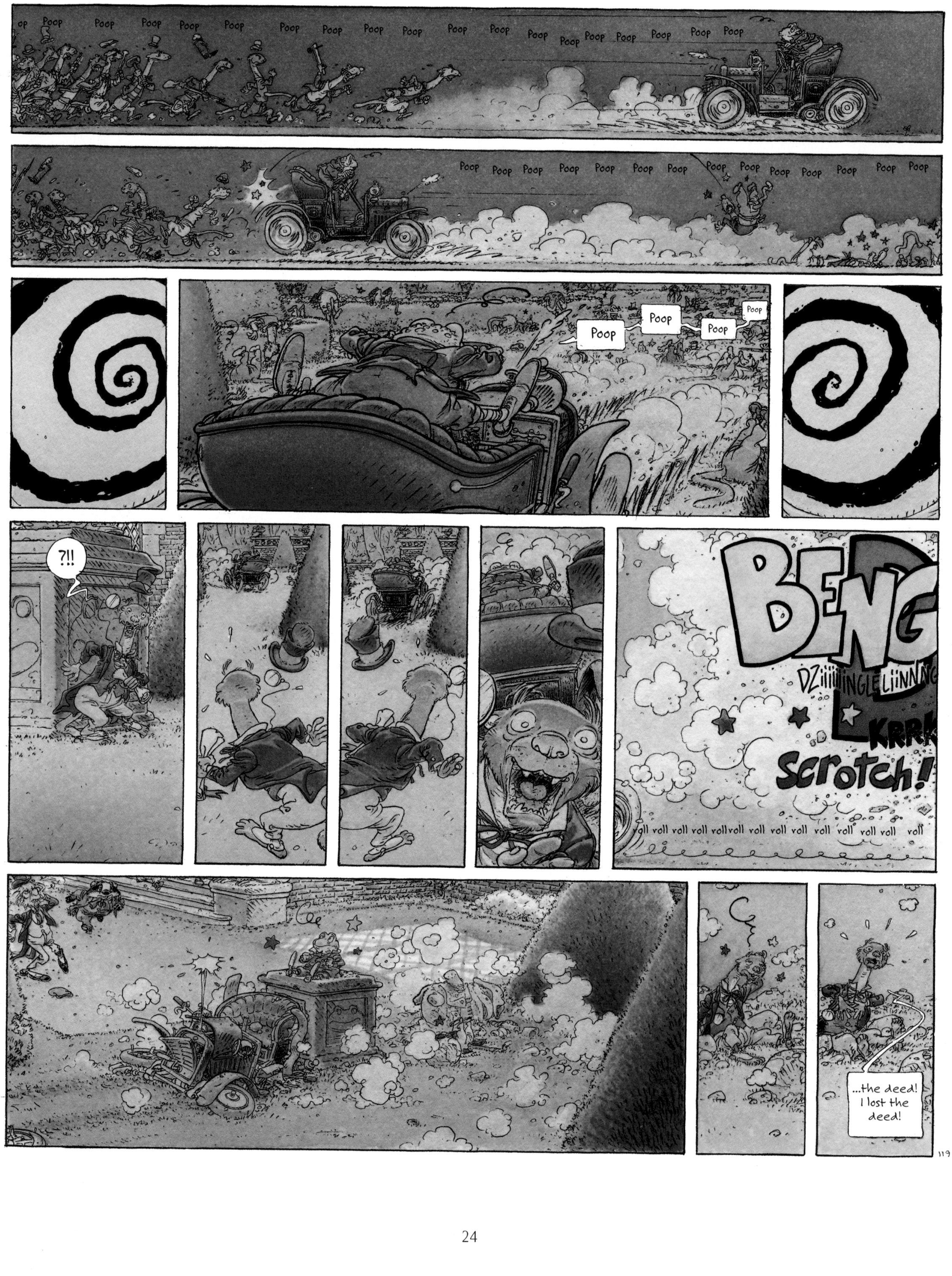
Poop Poop Poop Poop Poop Poop Poop Poop Poop Poop Poop Poop Poop Poop Poop Poop Poop Poop
Poop Poop Poop Poop Poop Poop Poop Poop Poop Poop Poop Poop Poop Poop
Poop
Poop
Poop
Poop
?!!
BENG
DZiiiiiiINGLE LiiNNNG
KRRK
Scrotch!
voll voll voll voll vollvoll voll voll voll voll voll voll voll voll
...the deed! I lost the deed!

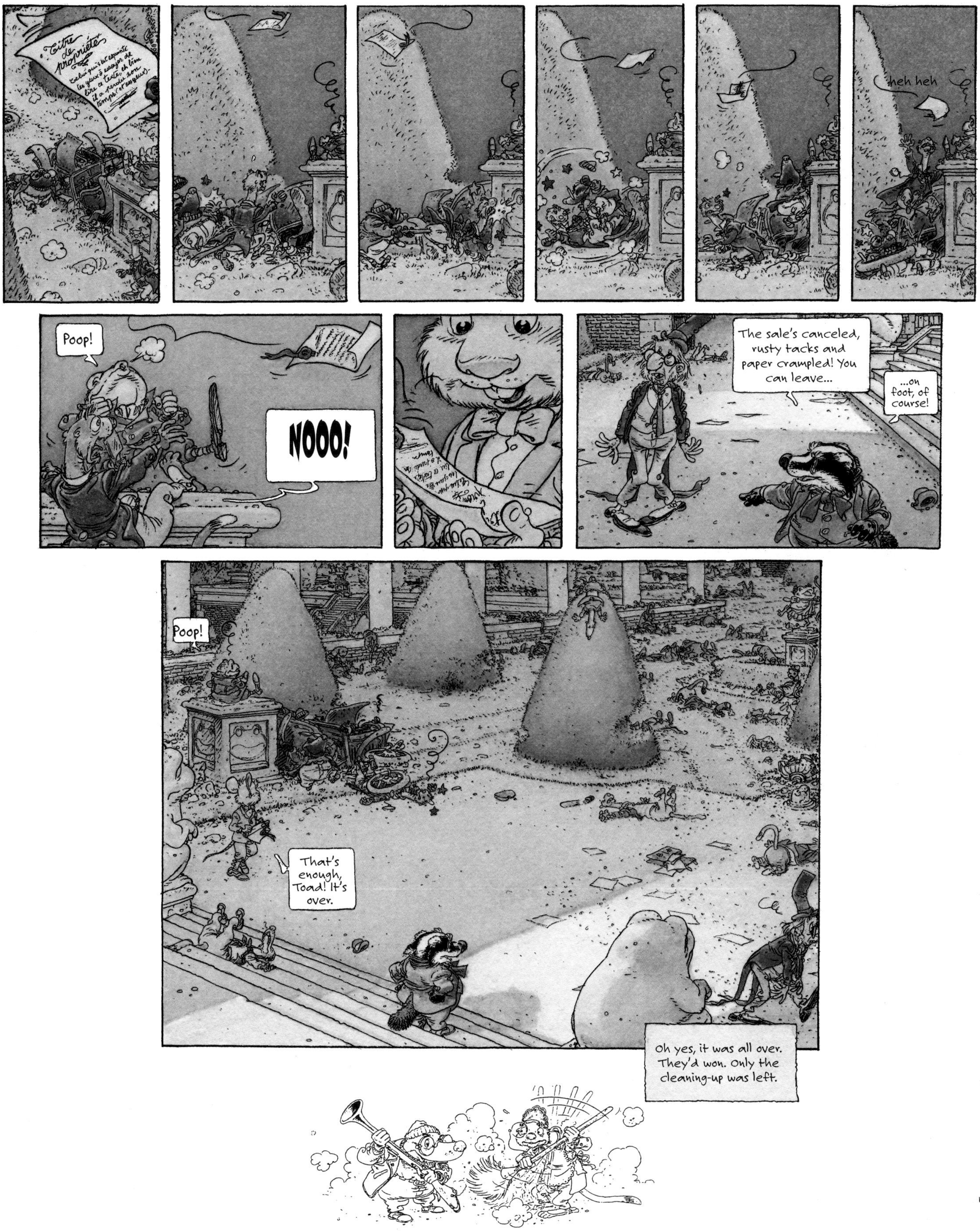
Titre de propriétés
heh heh
Poop!
NOOO!
The sale's canceled, rusty tacks and paper crampled! You can leave...
...on foot, of course!
Poop!
That's enough, Toad! It's over.
Oh yes, it was all over. They'd won. Only the cleaning-up was left.

Epilogue

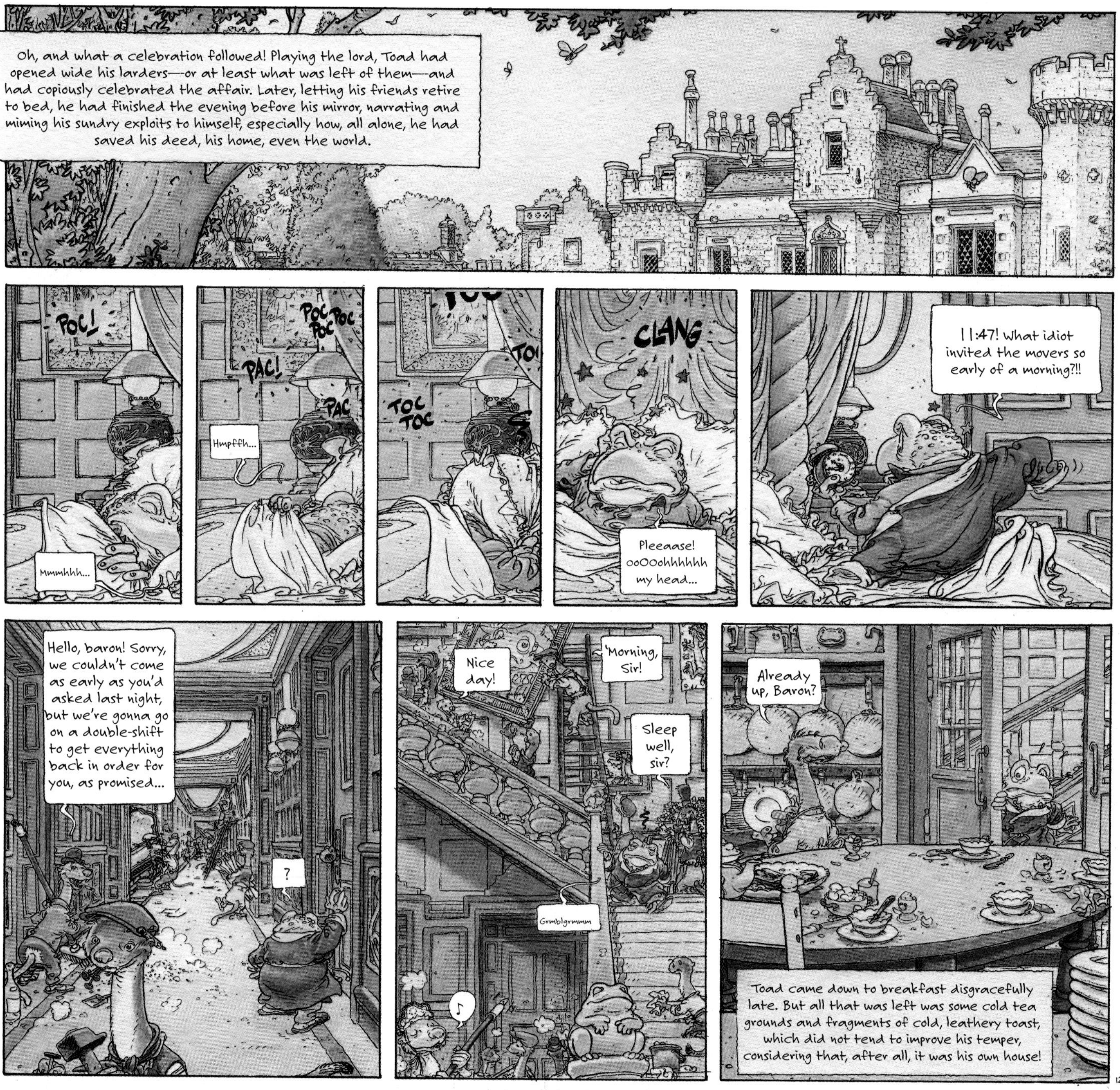

Oh, and what a celebration followed! Playing the lord, Toad had opened wide his larders—or at least what was left of them—and had copiously celebrated the affair. Later, letting his friends retire to bed, he had finished the evening before his mirror, narrating and miming his sundry exploits to himself, especially how, all alone, he had saved his deed, his home, even the world.
POC!
Mmmhhh...
POC POC POC
PAC!
PAC
Hmpffh...
TOC TOC
CLANG
Pleeaase! ooOOohhhhhh my head...
11:47! What idiot invited the movers so early of a morning?!!
Hello, baron! Sorry, we couldn't come as early as you'd asked last night, but we're gonna go on a double-shift to get everything back in order for you, as promised...
?
Nice day!
'Morning, Sir!
Sleep well, sir?
Grmblgrmmm
Already up, Baron?
Toad came down to breakfast disgracefully late. But all that was left was some cold tea grounds and fragments of cold, leathery toast, which did not tend to improve his temper, considering that, after all, it was his own house!

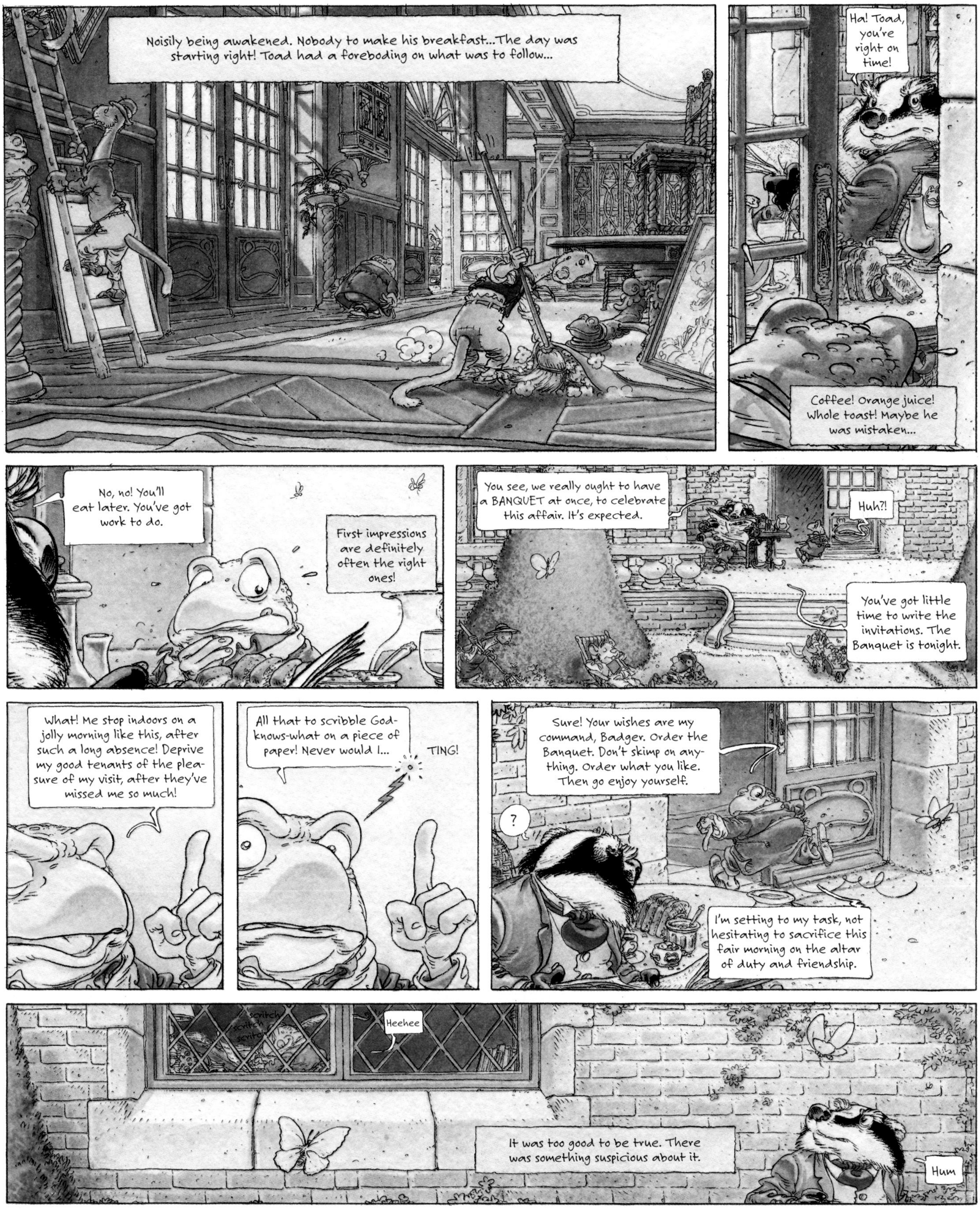
Noisily being awakened. Nobody to make his breakfast...The day was starting right! Toad had a foreboding on what was to follow...
Ha! Toad, you're right on time!
Coffee! Orange juice! Whole toast! Maybe he was mistaken...
No, no! You'll eat later. You've got work to do.
First impressions are definitely often the right ones!
You see, we really ought to have a BANQUET at once, to celebrate this affair. It's expected.
Huh?!
You've got little time to write the invitations. The Banquet is tonight.
What! Me stop indoors on a jolly morning like this, after such a long absence! Deprive my good tenants of the pleasure of my visit, after they've missed me so much!
All that to scribble God-knows-what on a piece of paper! Never would I...
TING!
Sure! Your wishes are my command, Badger. Order the Banquet. Don't skimp on anything. Order what you like. Then go enjoy yourself.
?
I'm setting to my task, not hesitating to sacrifice this fair morning on the altar of duty and friendship.
scritch
scritch
scritch
Heehee
It was too good to be true. There was something suspicious about it.
Hum
122

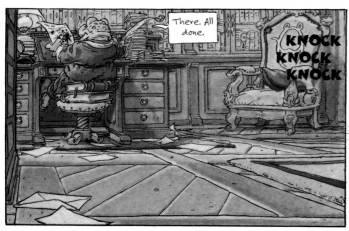

There. All done.
KNOCK KNOCK KNOCK
'Scuse me, Baron sir...I came to see if you'd like a drop of port before the meal...
As long as you're there, you can do me a small favor. A few invitations need to be delivered.
Excellent idea!
Toad came down almost on time to the dining room. He looked like someone flush with accomplishment.
Bon appétit, my friends!
Hic
A toast to a promising evening!
"Dear friend...
"...you have the signal fortune of being generously invited this evening by the very magnanimous Toad. Listed is the programme of entertainment that will ornament this extraordinary Banquet: Speech By Toad (There will be other speeches by Toad during the evening.) Address By Toad Synopsis—Our Prison System and judicial abuse—The Waterways of Old England and its implications in horse-dealing—Property, its rights and duties—On automobile driving and its role in the defense of property and individuals..."
PFttch!
Song By Toad (Composed by himself.) Short speech in honor of the master of the house By Toad Final Remarks By Toad
Where...where did you get that?!! I just gave them to...
Dear friend, you have the signal fortune of being generously invited this evening by the very magnanimous TOAD.
...a weasel. I know. I'm the one who sent him to you. I distrusted the gleam I saw in your eye. Once and for all, understand that there are going to be no speeches and no songs. We're not arguing with you; we're just telling you.
The good Mole is now sitting in the blue boudoir, filling up plain, simple invitation cards.
Just one little song...
NOOOM
...okay.
O dear, O dear, this is a hard world!
123

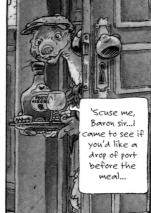

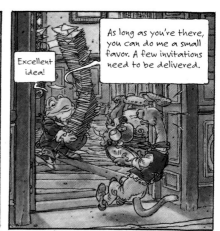

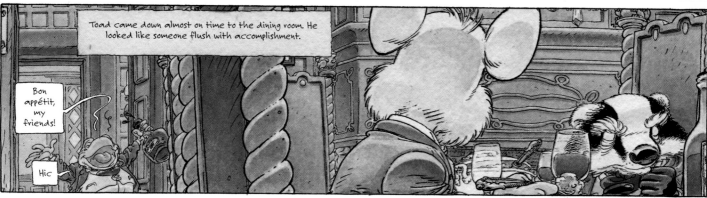

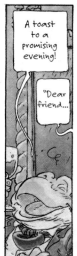

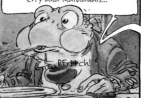

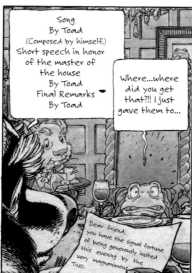

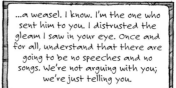

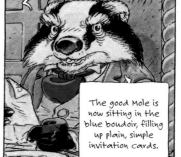

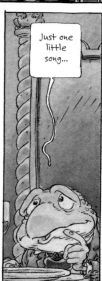

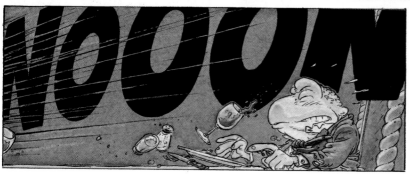

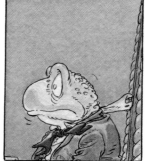

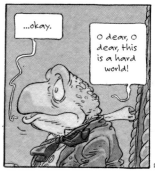

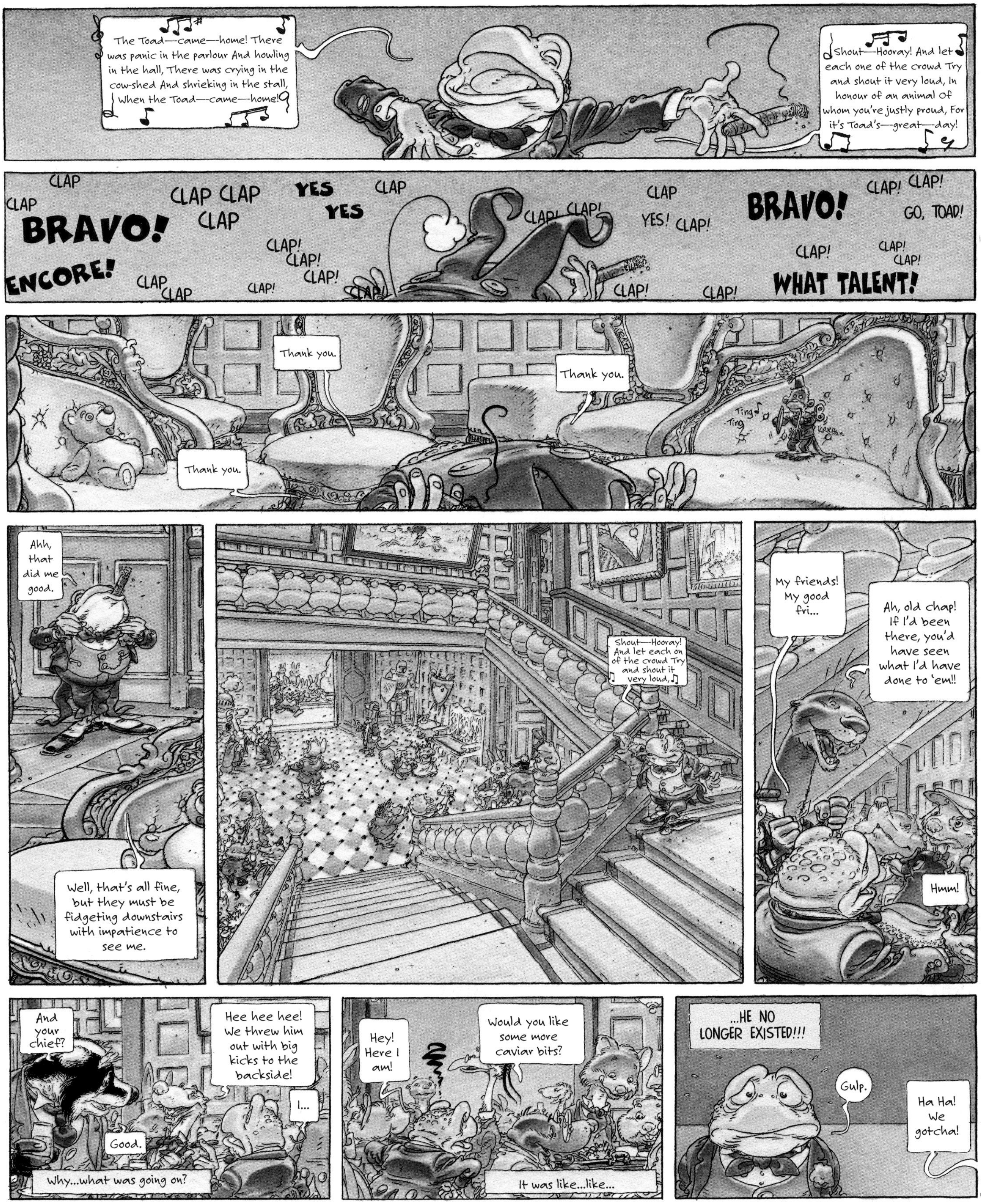

The Toad—came—home! There was panic in the parlour And howling in the hall, There was crying in the cow-shed And shrieking in the stall, When the Toad—came—home!
Shout—Hooray! And let each one of the crowd Try and shout it very loud, In honour of an animal Of whom you're justly proud, For it's Toad's—great—day!
CLAP CLAP
BRAVO!
ENCORE!
CLAP CLAP
CLAP CLAP CLAP
YES YES
CLAP!
CLAP! CLAP! CLAP!
CLAP!
CLAP!
CLAP! CLAP!
CLAP!
YES! CLAP!
CLAP!
BRAVO!
CLAP! CLAP!
GO, TOAD!
CLAP!
CLAP! CLAP!
CLAP!
WHAT TALENT!
Thank you.
Thank you.
Thank you.
Ting Ting
Ahh, that did me good.
Well, that's all fine, but they must be fidgeting downstairs with impatience to see me.
Shout—Hooray! And let each on of the crowd Try and shout it very loud,
My friends! My good fri...
Ah, old chap! If I'd been there, you'd have seen what I'd have done to 'em!!
Hmm!
And your chief?
Hee hee hee! We threw him out with big kicks to the backside!
I...
Good.
Why...what was going on?
Hey! Here I am!
Would you like some more caviar bits?
It was like...like...
...HE NO LONGER EXISTED!!!
Gulp.
Ha Ha! We gotcha!

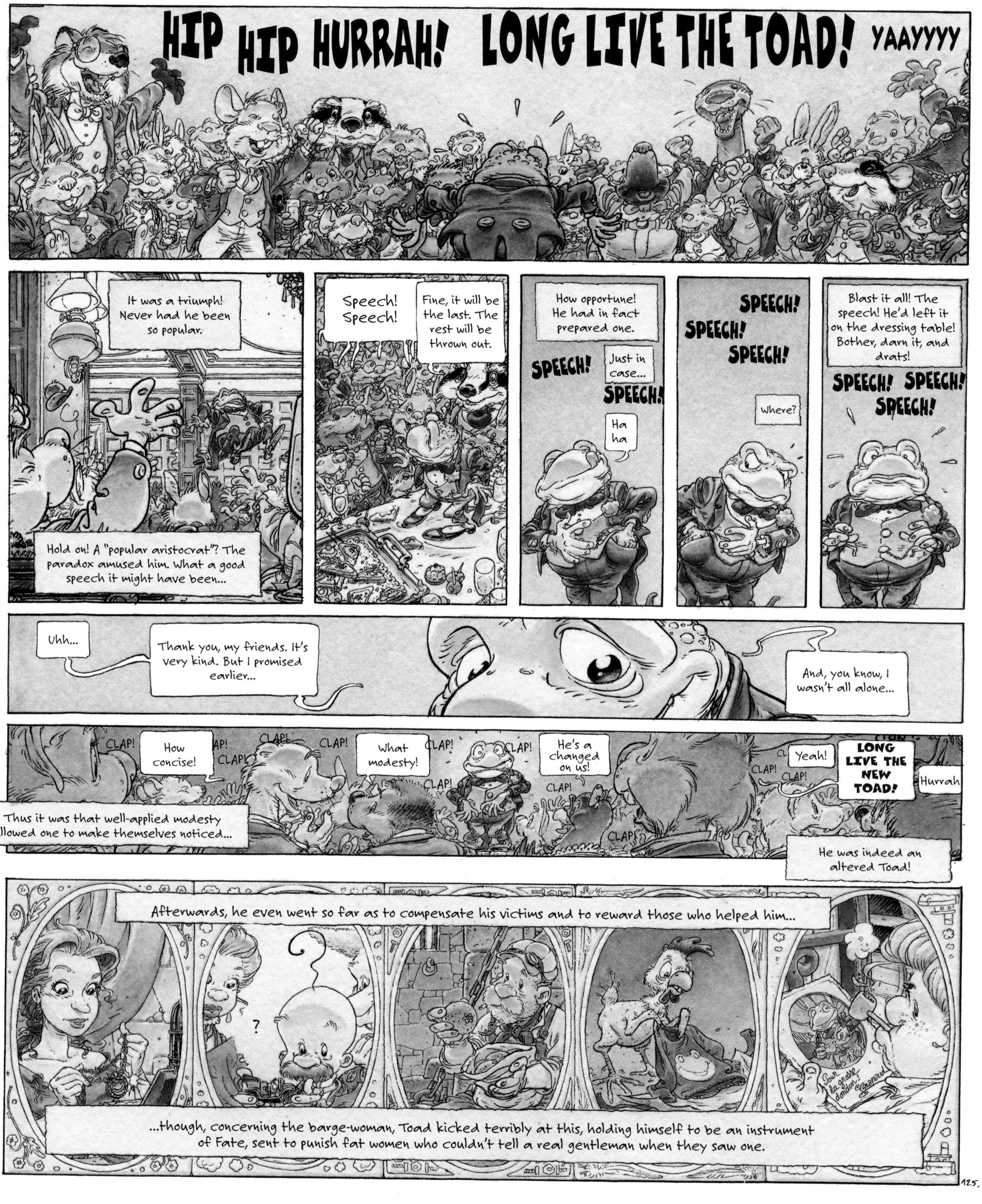

HIP HIP HURRAH! LONG LIVE THE TOAD! YAAYYYY
It was a triumph! Never had he been so popular.
Hold on! A "popular aristocrat"? The paradox amused him. What a good speech it might have been...
Speech! Speech!
Fine, it will be the last. The rest will be thrown out.
How opportune! He had in fact prepared one.
SPEECH!
Just in case...
SPEECH!
Ha ha
SPEECH!
SPEECH!
SPEECH!
Where?
Blast it all! The speech! He'd left it on the dressing table! Bother, darn it, and drats!
SPEECH! SPEECH! SPEECH!
Uhh...
Thank you, my friends. It's very kind. But I promised earlier...
And, you know, I wasn't all alone...
Thus it was that well-applied modesty allowed one to make themselves noticed...
CLAP!
How concise!
CLAP!
What modesty!
CLAP!
He's a changed on us!
Yeah!
LONG LIVE THE NEW TOAD!
Hurrah
He was indeed an altered Toad!
Afterwards, he even went so far as to compensate his victims and to reward those who helped him...
?
...though, concerning the barge-woman, Toad kicked terribly at this, holding himself to be an instrument of Fate, sent to punish fat women who couldn't tell a real gentleman when they saw one.

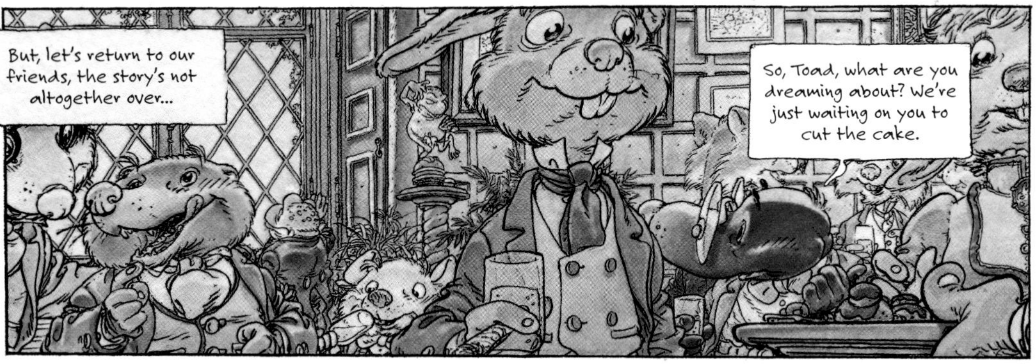
But, let's return to our friends, the story's not altogether over...
So, Toad, what are you dreaming about? We're just waiting on you to cut the cake.

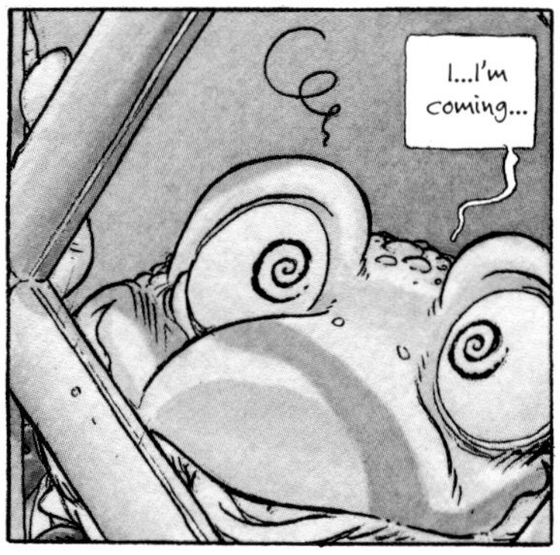
I...I'm coming...

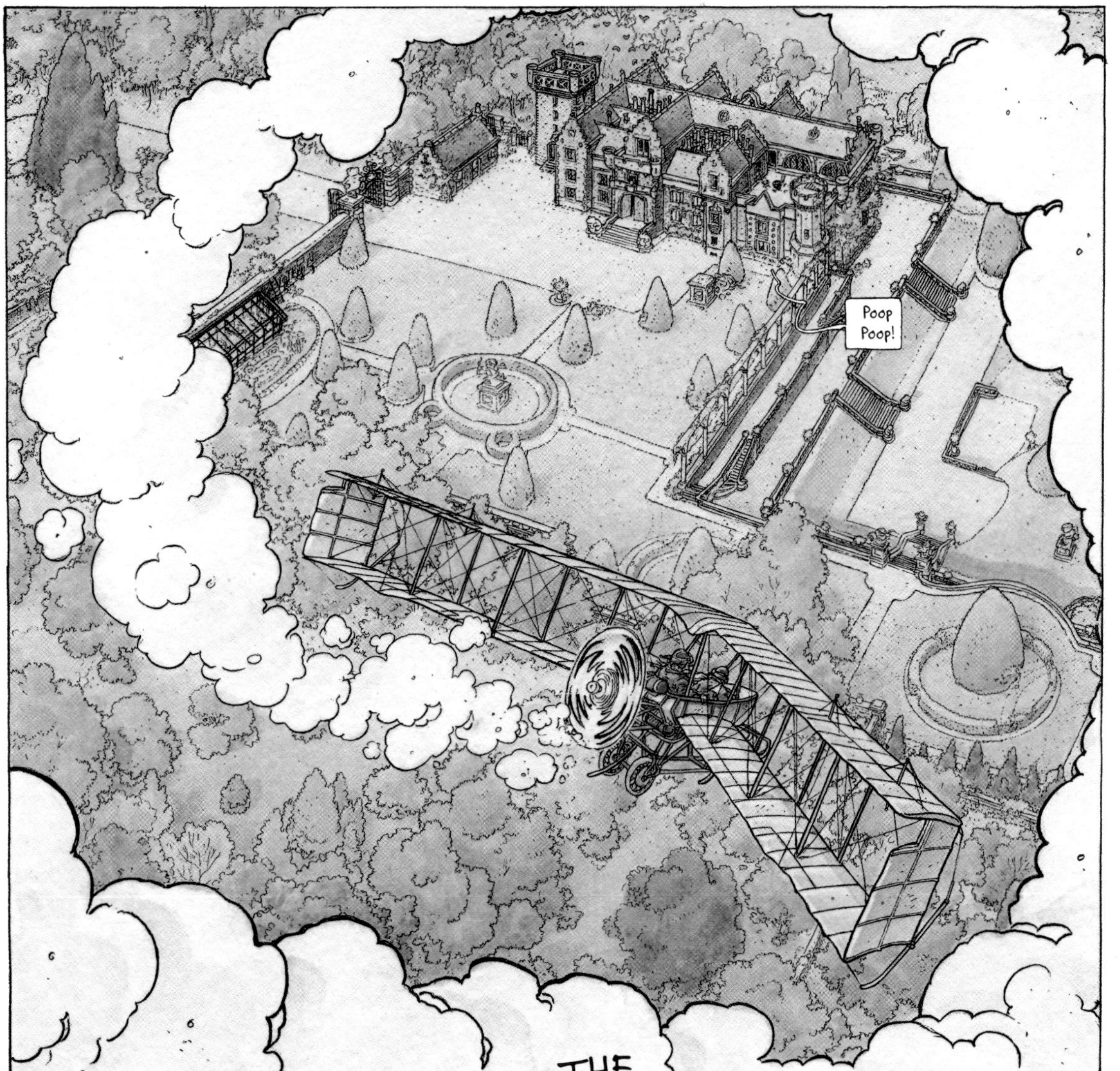
Poop Poop!

THE

END

michel Plessix with the friendly participation of Loic Jouannigot on the Mole's pads.
March '95-July 2001
Essaouira, Tinos, Etables s/mer, Las Tiolas, Rennes.